WAR AGAINST THE PLANET

SIGNPOST

ISSUES THAT MATTER

VIJAY PRASHAD

War Against the Planet

THE FIFTH AFGHAN WAR, IMPERIALISM, AND OTHER ASSORTED FUNDAMENTALISMS

LeftWord

Other titles in the series

SIGNPOST 1 N. Ram, *Riding the Nuclear Tiger*
SIGNPOST 2 Praveen Swami, *The Kargil War*
SIGNPOST 3 A.G. Noorani, *The RSS and the BJP: A Division of Labour*
SIGNPOST 5 A.G. Noorani, *Islam and Jihad*
SIGNPOST 6 Prabir Purkayastha and Vijay Prashad, *Enron Blowout: Corporate Capitalism and Theft of the Global Commons*
SIGNPOST 7 Vijay Prashad, *Namaste Sharon: Hindutva and Sharonism under US Hegemony*
SIGNPOST 8 Archana Prasad, *Environmentalism and the Left: Contemporary Debates and Future Agendas in Tribal Areas*
SIGNPOST 9 Prakash Karat, *Subordinate Ally: The Nuclear Deal and India–US Strategic Relations*
SIGNPOST 10 Prabir Purkayastha, Ninan Koshy and M.k. Bhadrakumar, *Uncle Sam's Nuclear Cabin*

Offset edition first published January 2002
Digital print edition March 2020

LeftWord Books
2254/2A Shadi Khampur
New Ranjit Nagar
New Delhi 110008
INDIA

LeftWord Books is a division of
Naya Rasta Publishers Pvt. Ltd.

ISBN 978-81-87496-19-9

Typset in Garamond and BankGothic

Contents

Acknowledgements

Much of this book was written in article form during the war and published by ZNET (thanks to Mike Albert), *Counterpunch* (thanks to Jeffrey St. Clair and Alexander Cockburn), *Outlook* (thanks to Sundeep Dougal), *Frontline* (thanks to P. Jacob and N. Ram), *Internazionale* (thanks to Giovanna Chioini), *Marxistische Blätter* (thanks to Ravi Ahuja), *Colorlines* (thanks to Tram Nguyen), *Economic and Political Weekly* (thanks to Bharati Bhargava), Black Radical Congress newslist (thanks to Art McGee), *Hartford Courant* (thanks to Carolyn Lumsden) and *Between the Lines* (thanks to Toufic Haddad). The book was written in conversation with Lisa Armstrong, Sudhanva Deshpande, Andy Hsiao, Biju Mathew, Sangeeta Kamat, Brinda Karat, Prakash Karat, Mike Karmody, Justin Podur, Raja Harish Swamy, Mark Toney and Bob Wing.

1

Introduction

The Fifth Afghan War (2001) is now over, or at least if we can trust the tenor of the four wars before this, it is over for the moment. The first three wars,[1] known as the First, Second and Third Anglo-Afghan Wars (1839–42; 1878–80; 1919) ended with agreements of peace and fellowship, but each of these resulted in further assaults mainly by the British through the Bolan and Khyber passes into the plains and highlands of Afghanistan. Afraid of Napoleon's presence in Persia and the southern encroachment of the Tsarist Empire, the British tried in 1839 to set up a former king of the Durrani royal family, Shah Shuja, over the fractious political landscape. But, after an early success in Kabul, the British imperial army was routed; it demolished the central bazaar and citadel of Kabul and retreated to the Punjab. As the guiles of diplomacy between the British, the Russians and the Durrani kings, what we know as the Great Game, intensified, Amir Sher Ali broke relations with the British in 1878 and waited for the British to enter his territory through the Bolan Pass. The Amir, in a classic Afghan warfare technique, fled Kabul for Mazar-e-Sharif, to await the departure of the

British (he died there not long afterwards). Again the people of Afghanistan rebelled against the British occupation and forced the retreat of the army back to Punjab. Active diplomacy and a show of force by the British forced the demarcation of the line that separated the British Empire from the Durrani Kingdom; known as the Durand Line, it was drawn in 1893 right through the homeland of the Pashtu speakers and has remained a bone of contention ever since. While the powers came to terms in the Anglo-Russian Convention (1907), the Durrani regime tried to gain some measure of independent action for the landlocked Afghan economy. The Third Afghan War of 1919 ended with the grant of formal independence to the country under the rule of Amir Amanullah.

After a long period of internal struggle between the monarchy and those who favoured a constitutional democracy, Amanullah's grandson, King Zahir Shah responded to popular pressure from his subjects with a constitution in 1964 and initiated a process known as 'New Democracy'.[2] The constitutionalists, the monarchists, the theocrats and the communists fought among each other until the latter took power in 1978. Splits in the Communist Party and pressure from the rebel theocrats led to the entry of Soviet troops in Afghanistan on 27 December 1979. The Fourth Afghan War began, then, between those who took the side of the Soviets and those who took the side of the theocrats. This war continued (despite the Soviet withdrawal on 15 February 1989, after the death of over 243,900 people according to the leftist president Najibullah), and it came to an end in 1992 when the theocrats took power. A period of warlord-dominated civil war continued between the theocrats till the Taliban exerted its sway in 1996. Most warlords retreated into exile or else became a shadow of their former selves until the summer of 2001, when one of them, Ahmed Shah Masud, made his first trip overseas to meet the heads of the European Union and to ask for a European or US assault on the Taliban.

The attacks on the World Trade Center and the Pentagon

on 11 September 2001 by nineteen men provided the pretext for the Fifth Afghan War, by far the most one-sided war ever to take place on Afghan soil. But the most significant thing about the Fifth Afghan War is that it is not a war about Afghanistan. The government of the United Kingdom, which speaks in proxy for the US government, says that the war is about the al-Qa'ida (The Base) group that was set up by the sorts of people invited in 1986 by CIA Director William Casey to join in the jihad against the Soviet army in Afghanistan. These international jihadis came through groups such as Osama bin Laden's Islamic Salvation Foundation and with support from the Saudi royal family's trust, the Rabitat al-Alam al-Islami (Muslim World League). At the time, these jihadis came to be called the 'Afghan International'[3] (like the Communist International), but they are now generally known as the 'Afghan Arabs' or the 'Arab Taliban'. The Taliban must go, we are told, because only then will the 'Afghan Arabs' lose their shelter and therefore lose their ability to conduct acts of terror against US targets.

Why are the former allies of the US, the 'Afghan Arabs', now so averse to the US that they consider it to be *dallaj* or the anti-Christ? The answer is simple. The US government, since the 1950s, has drawn on various radical Islamic groups to undermine both the communist movement in west Asia and Africa, but also to significantly demolish the legitimacy of the pan-Arabist or Arab socialist political parties. The ideology of these groups is motivated less by theological questions than by a secular desire to win power for an Islamicate-type regime: what drives most of these movements is not the intricacies of Islam as faith, but the desire to create a theocratic state. This does not mean that there is nothing about Islam in the ideology of these groups, but that the groups represent tendencies far more expansive than Islam itself.

Lands that boast the bulk of the world's Muslim population once had vibrant socialist and progressive movements, but the mendacity of the CIA ended their social sway. Indonesia, the nation state with the largest Muslim population in the world, once also had the largest Communist Party (the PKI) outside the socialist bloc, but with assistance from the CIA the Indonesian right wing decimated the party (for example, during the 1965 coup that installed Suharto to the presidency, the right massacred half a million PKI cadre). Sudan, with the largest Communist Party in Africa, faced the guns of President Numayri, backed by the CIA. Both African and Asian states with large Muslim populations, therefore, once lived within the progressive dynamic of Third World socialism and communism. Certainly the egalitarianism of Islam must have created the overall ethos within which the left operated. However, other important factors include the left's premier role in the anti-colonial nationalist movements in both Africa and Asia. US alliances with the local right demolished these movements and opened the door for radical Islamic groups to organize among the newly deracinated working-class. Saudi Arabia did not have a large communist movement, but its people did organize left-oriented groups right up to the early 1970s and thereafter. Those who are now called the 'Afghan Arabs' made an alliance with the US at the urging of the Saudi royal family to destroy all those democratic forces that would undermine the authoritarian hold of the oil by an alliance of the US-based oil companies and the vast and corrupt royal families of the oil lands. The 'Afghan Arabs', having helped the US render a fatal blow to the left, have now turned against their paymasters. But their paymasters would not leave. In the Gulf the main issue is protection of the oil-fields, and in Afghanistan the issue is both the protection of the Saudi regime (by the decimation of their principal opposition) and to smooth the way for the construction of oil and natural gas pipelines from Central Asia to South Asia (bypassing the far cheaper route through a virtually blockaded Iran).

Here the issue is mainly oil, but other interests also motivate the US army (itself the strong-arm of imperialist globalization). The Fifth Afghan War will allow the US to set up permanent bases in Uzbekistan and perhaps in northern Afghanistan; the

Kosovo campaign allowed the US to push NATO eastwards, despite the Russian reticence about this; the 'War on Drugs' in Colombia allows the US to have a permanent presence in South America and to run a retrofitted version of Operation Condor from its perch in that northern state; the naval alliances set up with states of the Pacific rim allow the US to threaten China from forward bases, to gnaw at the patience of the Chinese military and to prevent the reunification of Taiwan with the People's Republic of China (PRC); finally, the campaign for a missile defence shield is precisely not about defence, but about the deployment of weapons in space, about what the Pentagon calls 'Full Spectrum Domination'.[4] On 13 December 2001, as the war in Afghanistan wound to a close, President Bush gave formal notice that the US will withdraw from the Anti-Ballistic Missile Treaty (1972), because, he said, 'the ABM treaty hinders our Government's ability to develop ways to protect our people from future terrorist or rogue state missile attacks.' Russian President Vladimir Putin responded, 'This step was not a surprise to us. However, we consider it a mistake.' It was not a surprise because it is only one part of a well-laid out game plan for the assertion and maintenance of US hegemony across the planet and in the stars. These are the elements of the War Against the Planet, and one piece of it is the Fifth Afghan War, which is the subject of this brief book.

The book comes to you in three chapters. The first (9/11) offers a brief summary of the events that transpired in the United States on 11 September 2001 and afterwards. While Osama bin Laden may have been the mastermind of the events of that day, the question that needs to be asked is why did the US go after the Taliban and pay little heed to the Saudi regime (the bulk of the suicide bombers and bin Laden himself come from Saudi Arabia and not from Afghanistan)? Having raised that question, the second chapter (War in Passive Voice) offers a brief look at the war itself, but not the minutae of the military campaign. The questions raised here are of two sorts: first, what are the war aims of the US, and second, what does aerial bombardment accomplish that other forms of military engagement do not? Why was the US interested in the replacement of the Taliban, when in 1996 they had another reaction to its accession to power? What did the US hope to gain by bombardment from 30,000 feet? The question of war aims leads, once again, to the problem of Saudi Arabia. In the third chapter (Tolerance of Arabia), there are at least two points that I seek to establish: first, why does the US seek to protect the Ibn Saud family that rules Saudi Arabia, and second, how did the Islamicist groups come to hold such a prominent place in the politics of the Arab world? The obvious answer is the place of oil in our modern world, and this is what I explore in some measure. But capitalism's addiction to oil is only a part of the story: the diabolical history recounted here is also about the US fear of the left and the left's desire to use raw materials like oil for the people's benefit rather than for the voraciousness of capital.

2

9/11

I. NOTHING GOOD COMES FROM TERROR

All our emotions amount to cliché. The attacks on the World Trade Centres (WTC) brought grief not only to those who live in the United States, but also to families across the world. New York is a global city, and the sadness was equally global. Families from around the globe tried to reach the small island, grasping for any news of relatives who work in the area around the WTC, indeed who work anywhere in Manhattan – janitors, security guards, businesspeople, food vendors, and so many others. From Trinidad, India, Egypt, England, Bangladesh, Japan – there was not a country in the planet that did not have its telephone circuits to 001 – busy all day and into the night, and the days afterwards. The attack was on US soil, but it was also an attack on people of all kinds, from all corners of the world. In that sense, the event of 9/11 (the 11th of September, which, as 911 is the US telephone number for emergencies) was only partly an 'attack on America' (as the media and the Bush administration put it).

Nineteen Arab men, from Egypt, the United Arab Emirates and Saudi Arabia brought their various frustrations onto four commercial aircraft, three of which struck the WTC (in New York) and the Pentagon (in Washington, DC) – symbols of US global hegemony. Set on sixteen acres of land that was once the electrical district of New York and part of the vibrant working-class world of its port, the WTC stood at 1350 feet and was made up of over two hundred thousand tons of steel as well as four hundred and twenty five thousand cubic yards of concrete. About fifty thousand workers normally took up the twelve million square feet of office space within the WTC from the day the buildings opened in 1970, but on the morning of 9/11, the number was less than four thousand. Now the WTC is reduced to a seven-story pile of rubble.

Now, months after 9/11, there are still few details about the acts and its perpetrators even as we know intimate details about the thousands who died on that day (*The New York Times* carried a daily blotter, with a photograph, of the victims, to give us a sense of their lives). Of the nineteen Arab men we know little except that fourteen or fifteen of them came from Saudi Arabia and that the Egyptian leader, Mohammed Atta, held a Saudi passport. The US government promised a White Paper, but instead we only heard from the government of the United Kingdom who placed scanty evidence on their website to encourage us that the war that was inevitable was also just. No confession or final letter exists, as far as we know, that gives us a sense of what the nineteen men intended by their actions. Those who knew them are dumbfounded, since at least half of them did not evince anti-American or radical political Islamic ideals. What we do know is that these men are not from among the wretched of the earth, the hungry and desolate who have no options left in the world but to go out with a bang, to do something desperate as to kill thousands. Suicide bombers, thus far, mainly conform to this type, the forlorn Palestinian or Sri Lankan Tamil who is without moorings in organized politics and is seduced into suicide by crafty operatives of the militant right.

These nineteen men, however, came from among the

educated middle-class, with access to European technical education and with a reasonably bright future before them. And yet, they turned away from bourgeois tedium for a terrible martyrdom. The targets these men chose lead us to believe that the act was against the symbols of US imperialism, for these are the financial (WTC) and military (Pentagon) headquarters of neoliberal globalization. The problem with abstract domination, however, is that there is no one enemy, there is no centre that can be easily identified as the hub of global woes, there is no baron's castle or even industrialist's factory to assault. Domination, in this period of capitalism, is silent and faceless, but its tentacles squander the dreams of most of us across the world. We don't know why the nineteen men drove the planes to such terror, but perhaps they were in search of an enemy that made them feel less than human, that pushed them to squander their own ethics.

Only a few people on the world stage welcomed these attacks, for most of us condemned them without reservation. Before the enormity of 9/11 reached parts of the world some people did celebrate 9/11 as the comeuppance of US power, but this was retracted when it became clear that the scale of 9/11 far outweighs what has become routine say in Israel–Palestine or else in Northern Ireland or indeed in Sri Lanka. Quickly the international mood turned toward grief and many wondered how anyone could have been so callous as to do this deed. US President Bush did not help matters when he spoke of the men as Evil, when he dismissed any attempt to understand the social forces that drive people to such actions. If the actors are adjudged to be Evil, then there is no way to deal with them but to destroy them – to grant that they may be misguided in their strategy and tactics, but that they may represent a genuine grievance was tantamount to heresy. One can condemn an act without reservation, and *yet* attempt to analyse the act to see how it can happen. Analysis is not a justification, but a method to determine the causes of an act. To render the nineteen men and those who helped them as Evil allowed the US to forgo any discussion of the reasons why these men chose to attack symbols of US power. These nineteen men probably represent the frustrated and alienated human beings hemmed in by forces that are anonymous and that could only be embodied by these structures. The people who work in the WTC became the 'collateral damage' that we hear so much about when the US government's cruise missiles strike the innocent of the Third World. Those who died on 9/11 are martyrs of the US government's insane foreign policies, as well as martyrs of the insanity of neoliberal globalization, and those who brought them to their death were men misguided about the nature and art of political action.

Random acts of terror do not change anything for the better; indeed they increase the suffering of ordinary people. Right after 9/11, US pundits began to compare it to Pearl Harbor, the attack of the Japanese armed forces on 7 December 1941 that brought the US into World War II. President F.D. Roosevelt then called it a 'day of infamy', and this was the phrase that many used to describe 9/11. But, as Russian social scientist Boris Kagarlitsky put it, the more apt analogy for 9/11 is the burning of the Reichstag (the 1933 Nazi pretext for Hitler's seizure of power over the German state).[1] The only ones that will gain from 9/11's type of act are the radical right-wing forces in the advanced industrial states and in those countries that will once more bear the onus of the assorted fundamentalisms that plague the Third World – those political actors, funded often enough by their corrupt regimes, that reduce the ills of the world to eschatology and send young people to their deaths. Meanwhile, within the US, 9/11 enabled the right to refashion the compact between the people and the state so that both corporations and the political police (the Federal Bureau of Investigations, the FBI) encroached upon the freedoms of the individual. Immigrants and those who look like terrorists bore a disproportionate burden of the domestic measures. On the global stage, the United States has drawn together an alliance, however fragile, against terrorism. Germany and Japan seek to reinstate an active military force; the United Kingdom emerged as the great headmaster sent to cane a few old boys for straying from the rules of cricket; and finally, most regimes around the world take advantage of the 'war on terrorism' to deal with internal dissension of all sorts – whether this be the Colombian government's attempt to colour the Revolutionary Armed Forces of Colombia (FARC) with the reproach of terrorism, or Nepal's King Gyanendra's declaration of emergency rule to thwart the Communist Party of Nepal (Maoist) after their unwise attack on an army post, again in the name of anti-terrorism, or else the general wave of arrests in Europe against those who are part of some known Islamic-oriented terror networks, but also against those who are part of dissident groups who want to produce republics in the authoritarian gulf emirates.

Nothing good comes from terror. It never did and it never will.

II. BIN LADEN: DEAD OR ALIVE?

The first issue of New York's *Village Voice* after 9/11 ran with just one word emblazoned on a black cover, *Bastards*. The *New York Post* printed a picture of Osama bin Laden with the vigilante-cowboy justice phrase 'Dead or Alive' just beneath his chin ('Alive' was crossed out with a large X). The Bush administration, hours after the attacks, said 'Osama bin Laden and his al-Qa'ida organization were prime suspects', and CIA Director George Tenet pointed out by way of evidence that only bin Laden and his network had the capacity and tenacity to conduct 'multiple attacks with little or no warning'.

Osama bin Laden, the seventeenth son of the Yemeni construction magnate, Muhammad bin Laden (a close friend of King Ibn Saud, the founder of Saudi Arabia), is a ruthless man. There was a time when his callousness was useful to the CIA, as bin Laden brought scores of zealous anti-communist (and anti-modern) Arab men to Afghanistan to fight in CIA Director William Casey's 'jihad' against the Soviets and the leftist Afghan regime. As early as 1980 the United States government began to put pressure on Arab states to be more active in Afghanistan. Egyptian President Sadat announced that Egypt would help the cause because the Afghans 'are our Muslim brothers and in trouble'. The right wing radical Islamists, such as Ahmad Shawqi al-Istanbuli (the brother of Sadat's assassin and later one of bin Laden's senior associates), arrived in Afghanistan along with bin Laden (who came with the blessings of the Saudi royal family, via the Saudi intelligence chief Prince Turki bin Faysal). Saudi Arabia was eager to join the jihad, mainly to circumvent its encirclement by pro-Soviet forces (then in South Yemen and in the Horn of Africa). The royals had earlier asked bin Laden to form a 'volunteer' force in South Yemen along with the mujahideen constituted by Aden's last sultan, Tariq al-Fadli. Youssef Bodansky shows us that after the Yemeni expedition, the Saudi royals were so pleased with bin Laden that they personally gave him the contract to expand the Prophet's Mosque in Medina. A disinterested bin Laden refused the construction bid (it went to his family), but he personally asked King Fahd to support the jihad in Afghanistan. The King and his intelligence chief agreed, and bin Laden went off to south-central Asia as their unofficial envoy in the CIA–Saudi–ISI venture.[2] The CIA then saw his ruthlessness and his commitment to a severe form of Islam as an important asset.

Bin Laden's antipathy both to communism and to modernity was shaped into an armed militancy in Afghanistan, where, under the tutelage of the CIA and the ISI, he was able to learn the skills that have now allowed his network to grow. When Saddam Hussein entered Kuwait in 1990, bin Laden urged the Saudi royal family to allow the 'Afghan Arabs' a chance to join with the Saudi army in a campaign to remove the Iraqi army from Kuwait. When the US took leadership in the Gulf War and then when US troops remained in Saudi Arabia, this jihadi became incensed. His hatred of the US stems from this act: the permanent maintenance of troops in the birthplace of Islam. Expelled from Saudi Arabia, bin Laden arrived in Sudan to take shelter under the radical Islamic state of Hasan al-Turabi. Because of his anti-Saudi royal family stance and activities, the royals financially leaned on Sudan's ruler, General Bashir, who expelled bin Laden in May 1996. He then returned to Afghanistan, to create a base in the land controlled then by the Taliban. But it is crucial to underscore that even under the Taliban bin Laden was faced with restrictions against anti-Saudi activity and indeed against making provocative remarks. After the bombings of the US embassies in eastern Africa, the central leadership of the Taliban, it was reported, put bin Laden under house arrest in Kandahar and banned him from speaking to the media (a Taliban spokesperson did say, however, that bin Laden was being held for his own protection). Nevertheless on 20 August 1998, the US military fired cruise missiles both at Sudan and Afghanistan – nation-states that housed a renegade, but that themselves did not sponsor his activities. Without a doubt, bin Laden, a creation of the Saudi royals and the CIA, has created mayhem not only as an individual but also as a symbol for the creation of a violent network that includes groups around the planet.

Despite the unimpeachable evidence of bin Laden's activities, questions do remain about the nature of the Fifth Afghan War and the evidence proffered by the US–UK of the role of bin Laden *and the Taliban*.

Firstly, was bin Laden's culpability for 9/11 established before the US–UK bombardment of Afghanistan? This question is not specious nor does it apologize for bin Laden. On the contrary, such a line of enquiry has important implications for international relations and for the conduct of one state against another. After the December 2001 attack on the Indian parliament, the government of India used the US–UK example to threaten Pakistan with war, since it claimed, without any establishment of direct culpability, that Pakistan harbours terrorists. To attack without a firm chain of evidence creates international lawlessness.

What was the evidence by 7 October 2001, when the US–UK assault began? Neither the US nor the UK government offered a comprehensive account of bin Laden's guilt nor – and this is decisive – did we have an account of why the Taliban and Afghanistan should be a target of the US–UK onslaught. Three days before this, Prime Minister Tony Blair told the British parliament that the time for ultimatums had passed and that the Taliban had failed to hand over bin Laden in accordance with President George Bush's formula offered during a television address on the evening of 9/11: the United States government will 'make no distinction between the terrorists who committed those acts and those who harbour them'. The United Nations resolution 1373 made this logic the international norm in late September. The UK government's evidence against bin Laden, al-Qa'ida and the Taliban, as journalist Robert Fisk reported the next day, relied more 'on conjecture rather than on evidence'.[3] In fact, of the seventy points laid out by the document, only nine relate specifically to 9/11, while the rest report on the known history of al-Qa'ida and terror attacks against US targets, as well as on the heinousness of the Taliban – both well-known issues that do not, however, amount to even circumstantial evidence for the assaults of 9/11. Just because you have a criminal record does not make you guilty of any criminal act – the UK government's document, sanctified by the US government, dispatched all the basic norms of bourgeois legality. Indeed, the preface to the document notes that it 'does not purport to provide a prosecutable case against Osama bin Laden in a court of law. Intelligence often cannot be used evidentially due both to the strict rules of admissibility and to the need to protect the safety of sources. But on the basis of all the information available Her Majesty's Government is confident of its conclusions as expressed in this document.'[4] Certainly points 61 and 62 of the report point directly to al-Qa'ida (with bin Laden's statements to his associates prior to 9/11 that they leave Europe and that one of the nineteen men is a cadre of the organization), and the government notes that 'there is evidence of a very specific nature relating to the guilt of bin Laden and his associates that is too sensitive to release'. Like FBI Director Tenet, the UK government noted that 'Osama bin Laden and al-Qa'ida have the capability to execute major terrorist attacks'. The UK report lists three events that it says were a prelude to 9/11: the assault on

US soldiers in Somalia in October 1993 (18 dead); the bombing of the US embassies in Kenya and Tanzania in August 1998 (224 dead and 5000 injured); the attack on the USS Cole in Yemen in October 2000 (17 dead and 40 injured). The Somalia incident does not merit room on this list, mainly because the deaths of the US marines took place as troops of a Somali warlord shot down their helicopters in the middle of a US attack on the warlord's base (where pro-bin Laden 'Afghan Arabs' formed part of the warlord's army). This conflict was not a terrorist one by any definition. The United States government accuses bin Laden of the Kenya–Tanzania carnage, but it has not formally made this charge; in December 1998, bin Laden denied that he was involved in the attacks, but he did say that he 'instigated' them in retaliation for the US air strikes on Iraq. Finally, onto the USS Cole, where again the US government has not formally charged bin Laden, but another Saudi man, Muhammad Omar al-Harazi who remains in custody as a suspect in the case. It *is* conceivable that bin Laden masterminded all these acts, indeed that he helped raise the money for them, arrange the logistical details and find the manpower to conduct them. This is not in contention.

Indeed, on 13 December 2001, the US Military released a video tape that they found in a private residence in Jalalabad, just as news arrived via Abu Jaffer, a Saudi financier, that Osama bin Laden had fled Afghanistan. In the videotape, bin Laden meets with a Saudi man after 9/11, and offers what appears to be a candid confession for his role in 9/11. 'We calculated in advance the number of casualties from the enemy, who would be killed based on the position of the towers', he said almost gleefully. 'Due to my experience in the field, I was thinking that the fire from the gas in the plane would melt the iron structure of the building and collapse the area where the plane hit and all the floors above it only. That is all that we had hoped for', but, as he recounted to his Saudi associate, he and his network did not predict that the towers would collapse entirely. If bin Laden is to be believed, then indeed he is guilty of planning the horrendous events of 9/11 executed no doubt by a network that owes fealty to him.

The second question is this: why did the US–UK target Afghanistan in the attacks when the state did not itself participate in the events of 9/11? What has the Taliban to do with bin Laden, and should any state now be culpable for the acts of those who take refuge there, particularly if the state does not have an extradition treaty? Idi Amin, the deposed ruler of Uganda, lives in Saudi Arabia; if the Saudis refuse to hand him over to the Ugandan regime to be tried for his crimes in the early 1970s, can the Ugandan army enter the peninsula and get him? The Duvaliers live in France, would the Haitian army be justified in an assault on the beaches of Normandy? Does the US action repeal the international norms on extradition?[5] In the 1998 attacks, the US military targeted the bin Laden camps in Khost, mainly to send a message to the network that it would bear retribution for its acts. This time the US military followed the Israeli government's playbook: when Hamas or other groups that are based in the Palestinian Authority act within Israel, the Israeli Defense Force attacks PLO and Palestinian Authority targets with the logic that it wishes to inflict as much pain on the government as possible to make them act against Hamas and its kin groups. The Taliban failed to hand over bin Laden or to check his activities, so they had to feel the wrath of a thousand guns. But the US exceeded the Israeli brief: the point was not to force the Taliban to act, but it was to overthrow the Taliban and to put in place an administration pliant to US demands. The precedent set by this action is immense, for it now opens the door, for example, for an Israeli occupation of the PA and the creation of a puppet administration there (more so than Yasser Arafat's now generally conciliatory regime). The Taliban had to go not only because of bin Laden, but mainly for reason of oil that I shall go into below.

The third question that follows from this is what other interests and social forces are hidden by this massive act against the Taliban, a regime in place since 1996 and otherwise considered by the US to be fairly benign in international terms (it did not make the State Department's rogue state list, an indication that it may not have been an area of 'concern' for the US before late 2001)? Justice operates on two registers. First there is the need to establish the guilt of those who conducted (planned and executed) the acts of 9/11 and try them, perhaps in the International Court of Justice. Second, a violent act creates an immense amount of insecurity among the people who have the right to live in a secure world. To make people secure, it is the responsibility of the state and the international institutions to root out the cause of the violence. Bin Laden's confession suggests that he participated in the acts of 9/11, but to target him alone ignores the social forces that produced 9/11. Indeed, bin Laden's speech broadcast on 3 November by Al-Jazeera, the Arabic-language satellite television network (based in Doha, Qatar), suggests what some of these forces may include: 'The polls showed that the vast majority of the sons of the Islamic world were happy about these strikes [of 11 September] because they believe that the strikes were in reaction to the huge criminality practiced by Israel and the United States in Palestine and other Muslim countries'. In the tape released on 13 December, bin Laden asked his Saudi associate with great interest how the mosques in Saudi Arabia responded to 9/11 and he sat quietly as his visitor recounted the various statements of the leading clerics in Arabia. Bin Laden interjected to ask about this or that cleric, eager to see that his act had created an upsurge of anti-American sentiment in Arabia. The nineteen men who flew the planes came from Saudi Arabia, from Egypt, from the United Arab Emirates. Many of these men and their associates are financed by terror networks, some hidden in France and nurtured in Algeria, or else raised in the Gulf itself, educated in the generally anti-American Saudi schools and financed by renegade members of the Saudi Royal family (now numbering over ten thousand) many of whom fester in a vengeful brand of Islam and in their own descent into a petro-Babylonian captivity. If this is the case, then the second register of justice (to create security for the people's of the world) will not be gained by the wholesale bombardment of Afghanistan. Why did the Taliban and Afghanistan bear the weight of bin Laden, when he himself shows us that the Saudis are as implicated in these social forces as anyone else?

Indeed, the close relationship between a sizable section of the Saudi Royal family and the fundamentalism of the bin Laden type is well known to US intelligence and to policy makers. The US National Security Agency began to intercept conversations between members of the Saudi royal family since 1994 and, according to journalist Seymour Hersh, 'the intercepts depict a regime increasingly corrupt, alienated from the country's religious rank and file, and so weakened and frightened that it has brokered its future by channeling hundreds of millions of dollars in what amounts to protection money to fundamentalism groups that wish to overthrow it.'[6] Not only are the Saudis culpable by the Bush standard (they financed groups that may be part of the chain that executed 9/11), but they also put in place an educational system that promoted an anti-American sort of fierce Islam as a hedge to establish the royal family's credibility in the country at the same time as the royals begged for US assistance to maintain their deficits (an annual feature since 1983). The government, we are told by a non-partisan US think tank, 'tolerated a decline in educational standards in the name of Islam. The ulema have been allowed to increase their influence over the curriculum, and more and more students are encouraged to pursue Islamic studies, which do not offer any career opportunities and increase the disaffection of Saudi youth. The futility of such education is exemplified by a glut of [graduates] in Islamic studies whose degrees are not taken seriously by Islamic scholars in other Arab countries and who have often become opponents of the government that has educated them.'[7] A Saudi Ministry of the Interior report (1995) shows that as many as twelve thousand Saudi men from these types of institutions had spent time in paramilitary training (to become 'Afghanis'), and these men (the estimates go so high as twenty-five thousand) form the nucleus for potential militant organs that are opposed to the Saudi royal family's capitulation to US imperialism. The circumstantial evidence against the Taliban, then, is as strong as it is against the Saudi regime (who had a hand in the production of these men, mainly as an insurance policy for its own regime's ideological bind), and yet the US–UK does not go after the dynasty of Ibn Saud.

Despite the Bush administration's constant refrain about 'our Saudi friends', the Saudi regime has been reticent to allow any genuine investigation of violent events within Saudi Arabia and by Saudi nationals elsewhere. Hersh notes that 'the American intelligence officials have been particularly angered by the refusal of the Saudis to help the FBI and the CIA run "traces" – that is, name checks and other background information – on the nineteen men.' A senior member of the US intelligence community told Hersh that the Saudis may never allow the US to gain access to information about the men, mainly because the Saudis 'have only one constant – and it's keeping themselves in power'.

This is not the first time the Saudis have balked before full disclosure. On 13 November 1995 a large bomb killed seven people (five US nationals and two Indians) in the US Army Material Command's Office of the Programme Manager for the Saudi National Guard. Three unknown groups, the Movement for Islamic Change in the Arabian Peninsula-Jihad Wing, the Tigers of the Gulf and the Combatant Partisans of God took responsibility and demanded the withdrawal of US troops from Saudi Arabia. In a remarkable act of denial the Saudi Ambassador to the US, Bandar Bin Sultan Bin Abd al-Aziz wrote, 'dissidents did not cause the car bombings'.[8] The Saudi police arrested four men, three of whom had spent time in Afghanistan in the late 1980s, and beheaded them on 31 May 1996 without a protracted investigation that may have revealed the level of discontent within the kingdom. The Interior Ministry dismissed links to the three groups that had taken responsibility for the attack and it claimed that the men were agents of an unnamed foreign power, not dissidents. Much the same happened in the aftermath of the al-Khobar towers bombing (25 June 1996), where a large bomb killed nineteen US troops and injured three hundred and seventy three others who lived in these apartment buildings beside the US air base and down the road from the US oil installations at Dhahran. Close to the end of the year it became clear that the perpetrators of the attacks came from the ranks of Saudi Hezbollah, a group that draws from the Shi'a of eastern Saudi Arabia who are distressed by their decline in status since the 1970s as a result of Saudi and US oil policies. The Saudi regime hesitated to assist the US, and even as the US finally indicted thirteen Saudi militants of Hezbollah and one Lebanese chemist on 21 June 2001, the Saudi Interior Minister, Prince Nayef, said that 'no other entity has the right to try or investigate any crimes occurring on Saudi lands', and he denied the existence of Saudi Hezbollah. Saudi Defence Minister Prince Sultan noted, 'this issue concerns Saudi Arabia alone', just as President Bush thanked 'the Kingdom of Saudi Arabia for their assistance in this investigation'.[9]

The focus on bin Laden after 9/11 allows the US and the Saudi regime to deflect attention from the social history that produced the Saudi nationals who did convert the commercial aircraft into guided missiles. Bin Laden, meanwhile, seems to enjoy being at the centre of things, to be seen as the mastermind of forces that he cannot control even if he has become a symbol to groups around the world that draw their ideology from a severe form of Islam. His mystical language about the crusades only makes him seem more likely to be the arch-villain, the super-evil figure to the superman of Bush (bin Laden called Bush–Blair's war against the planet a 'fundamentally religious' conflict between the Muslims and 'the people of the West, who are the crusaders'). To pin 9/11 on bin Laden removes the need to investigate the life-stories of the nineteen men, to find out how it is that so many Saudis are dissatisfied with their condition, indeed why they seem to be unhappy with the presence of a permanent US military establishment in Saudi Arabia since the

Gulf War of 1990–91. Saudi reticence to investigate the attacks on US personnel from the 1991 attack on a shuttle bus in Jeddah (two US servicemen injured there) to 9/11 indicate, at most, the implication of a section of the royal family in the anti-US organizations and, at least, the presence of a disorganized, but militantly effective, dissent within Saudi Arabia that comes from the radical right, but which is informed by populist ideas about the better spread of the petro-profits.

Bush and bin Laden, both men of oil, talked of the war in religious terms. Bush, in the lead, made the conflict about bin Laden and the Taliban, when in fact the struggle should have proceeded from an investigation of 9/11 and then moved in two directions: toward the arrest and trial of those who assisted the suicide bombers, and then toward the reconfiguration of the causes that produced such horrid desperation in the first place. Security for all people cannot be purchased on the backs of a mirage, because the war against bin Laden produces no guarantee that such acts of terror will not occur in the future. Indeed, to go after bin Laden and the Taliban creates further instability in the world and obscures those grievances of a swath of the world's swarthy peoples that are so important to this story.

Bin Laden: Dead or Alive? Nothing else mattered, not least of which, Saudi Arabia and the international petro-mafia.

III. A FUEL'S ERRAND

Bin Laden and al-Qa'ida moved to Afghanistan in 1996 to take up home again in the valleys of southern Afghanistan that were once the bases of the mujahideen, and were built with CIA assistance in the war against the leftist regime, and later the Soviet army. The UK government, on their website charge sheet, alleged that the 'Taliban regime allows bin Laden to operate his terrorist training camps and activities from Afghanistan, protects him from attacks from outside, and protects the drug stockpiles. Osama bin Laden could not operate his terrorist activities without the alliance and support of the Taliban regime', therefore, if bin Laden must go, the Taliban must be taken out first. The departure of the Taliban is foremost, therefore, a means to get bin Laden.

Indeed, the United States government has had a very ambivalent relationship with the Taliban prior to 9/11. Shortly after the Taliban took power in Kabul on 27 September 1996, the United States State Department offered the following assessment: 'Taliban leaders have announced that Afghans can return to Kabul without fear, and that Afghanistan is the common home of all Afghans', said spokesperson Glyn Davies. The US felt, in addition, that the Taliban's assertion in Kabul would allow 'an opportunity for a process of reconciliation to begin'. Reconciliation was a pipe-dream, as the troops led by the Tajik warlord Ahmed Shah Masud and the troops led by the Uzbek general Abdul Rashid Dostum, as well as the Hazara-dominated Hizb-e-Wahdat party disturbed the vales of Afghanistan with warfare. The Taliban's entry into power seemed, even in Afghanistan, as a harbinger of peaceful times – when the Taliban forces routed Gulbuddin Hikmatyar's headquarters in Charasyab (14 February 1995) they broke a long economic blockage of Kabul conducted by that darling of the United States and Pakistan in his own small war against the other warlords. 'It was a popular step', wrote Pakistani journalist Ahmed Rashid, 'raising the Taliban's prestige amongst the skeptical citizens of Kabul'.[10] Despite their horrendous record on social matters, the Taliban initially appealed to some Afghan people whose lives had been in chaos since at least 1992 (when the leftist regime fell) if not since 1979 when the mujahideen–Marxist clash became a war.

But the real forces that took solace from the Taliban included the Pakistani government (for reasons that we will go over below), the transport mafia (because stability meant the protection of their convoys of heroin from Afghanistan into Pakistan and then to points beyond), the oil companies (because the Taliban seemed as eager as any regime to profit from its geo-strategic location for a natural gas and oil pipeline from Central

Asia to the Persian Gulf), and the United States government (eager for a friendly regime that would enable a US forward post against Iran, the PRC and Russia). Glyn Davies even said that the US found 'nothing objectionable' in the Taliban's social agenda, and Senator Hank Brown (a close supporter of the oil companies' bid to build the trans-Afghan pipeline) said that 'the good part of what has happened is that one of the factions at last seems capable of developing a government in Afghanistan'. All this followed two trips (one in April, the other in August of 1996) to Pakistan and Afghanistan by US Assistant Secretary of State for South Asia Robin Raphel where she said, 'We have an American pipeline company which is interested in building a pipeline from Turkmenistan through to Pakistan. This pipeline project will be good for Turkmenistan, for Pakistan and for Afghanistan as it will not only offer job opportunities but also energy in Afghanistan.'[11]

On 10 October 1996 the US State Department revised its analysis of the Taliban on the basis of sustained pressure from human rights and women's groups in the advanced industrial states as well as pressure from a regional conference held in Iran (India, among the participants, took a significant stand against the Taliban's social policies). 'We do not see the Taliban as the saviour of Afghanistan', said the State Department. 'We never really welcomed them'. The main reason offered for this was the Taliban's 'uniquely discriminatory manner' with women. Nevertheless, Robin Raphel noted in November, 'The Taliban control more than two-thirds of the country, they are Afghan, they are indigenous, they have demonstrated staying power. The real source of their success has been the willingness of many Afghans, particularly Pashtuns, to tacitly trade unending fighting and chaos for a measure of peace and security, even with severe social restrictions. It is not in the interests of Afghanistan or any of us here that the Taliban be isolated.'[12] In February 1997, a Taliban delegation visited Washington DC for talks with the State Department and with Unocal – the contact continued, and the US still pinned its hopes on the Taliban as a factor of stability for US interests in the region. The woes of the Afghan people seemed unimportant.

Afghanistan was largely forgotten on the world stage (that is, in the monopoly media) until the bombings of the US embassies in East Africa. Very quickly the US government charged the bombings to the account of bin Laden, a resident of Afghanistan after he had been asked to leave by the Sudanese government in 1996 (bin Laden lost his Saudi citizenship in 1994, had lived in Sudan since 1991 and had been ejected from there due to international pressure over his role in various terror networks). President Clinton, in a hurried response to the bombings, ordered the US military to fire seventy cruise missiles at bin Laden's camps near Khost and Jalalabad. Among the dead lay three men from Yemen, two from Egypt, one Saudi, one Turk, seven Pakistanis and twenty Afghans. A Pakistani group, Harkat-ul-Ansar, controlled one of the camps, called Al-Badr, whose purpose was to fuel insurgency in the Kashmir valley.[13] Bin Laden escaped unscathed. The Taliban protested this rash act by the US, one that violated all manner of treaties and disregarded the UN as an arbiter for justice in the world. Bin Laden, after 1998, became the US's symbol for international terrorism, much as Carlos the Jackal was once the dreaded symbol of terror in the 1970s, but even the US monopoly media was unsure about the inflation of bin Laden's role in terrorist violence around the world.[14] The Taliban, meanwhile, were bystanders to this process, even as they rearranged social life against the wishes of the Afghan people.

So why, after 9/11, did the US decide not only to go after bin Laden, but also to overthrow the Taliban regime? Certainly if the European press is to be believed, two CIA agents met with bin Laden as recently as July 2001 in Dubai when the ailing Saudi went to get a medical check-up for his collapsed kidneys. Sheltered in an American hospital, bin Laden, it is reported, met with the then Saudi Intelligence chief Prince Turki bin Faysal, who retired from that job in early September 2001 after twenty-five years' service, perhaps because of his relationship with bin Laden.[15] In addition, what may we make of the Track Two meeting in Berlin held by the powers in mid-July, just as the CIA met bin Laden in Dubai? The Pakistani envoy to that meeting reports that former US Ambassador Tom Simons informed the powers that the US has a new mode for an assault on Afghanistan. This new attack would succeed where Clinton's 20 August 1998 cruise missile attack (Operation Infinite Reach) failed. 'They had all the intelligence and would not miss [bin Laden] this time. It would be an aerial action, maybe helicopter gunships, and not only overt, but from very close proximity to Afghanistan'.[16] The game plan laid out in Berlin was followed precisely by the US in this most recent Afghan war. Bin Laden and the attack on the WTC, then, offer a pretext for the US to overthrow the barely legitimate Taliban, install a regime friendly to the US, push forward the Central Asian pipeline, and, if all goes well, perhaps ensure that a US-based transnational such as Unocal gets the contract rather than the Argentine transnational, Bridas. The war, after all, is a fuel's errand.

But this is not what we heard in the month between 9/11 and the start of the Afghan war. We heard that the war is about Civilization against Barbarism, even of a Clash of Civilizations, Modernity versus Islam. In the summer of 1993 Harvard University's Professor of Government Samuel Huntington wrote in *Foreign Affairs* that the 'fundamental source of conflict in this new world will not be primarily ideological or primarily economic. The great divisions among humankind and the dominating source of conflict will be cultural. Nation states will remain the most powerful actors in world affairs, but the principle conflicts of global politics will occur between nations and groups of different civilizations. The clash of civilizations will be the battle lines of the future.' Christian Modernity, he implied, is under threat from 'Confucian and Islamic states' and the role of the US must be to bolster the former against the latter.[17]

When Christian white supremacists act against Civilization,

or else when capitalist firms act against Civilization, these acts are reduced to the work of one man and not to an entire cultural world. When the police arrested Timothy McVeigh for the 1995 Oklahoma City bombing, no one talked of Christianity in crisis, even as McVeigh's white supremacists are guided by a Biblical fundamentalism and Aryanist racial theories. What about those headlines: Christianity in Crisis, Christianity Against Civilization. Crises of capitalism, too, do not get put in these general terms. We only hear about the depredations of this or that stockbroker (Harshad Mehta in India, the boy of Barings in Singapore, Jonathan Lebed in the US), or of this or that business collapse. Several large corporations (Boeing, the airline industry, Cisco Systems) fired over a lakh of workers and blamed this catastrophe on terrorism, but even this did not bring forth the headlines of my imagination: Capitalism Against Civilization, Profits Against People, the Crisis of Capitalism.

Bin Laden is the singular figure of hatred, but he has come to stand for radical Islam in general, if not Islam itself, and the assault on the Taliban and on 'terrorism' is used by states across the world to deal with the insurgencies of their populations who have turned to Islam as the main framework of struggle. If Islam-bin Laden is the civilizational problem, then there is little more analysis necessary. If Islam-bin Laden is the purported target, then we can forget that the war is about the protection of the Ibn Saud family's control over a quarter of the oil in the world; that the war is about the pipelines for Central Asian natural gas and oil through Afghanistan into South Asia; that the war is about an assault against the same radical political Islam that was once shepherded by the CIA; that the war allows the US to establish permanent bases in central Asia, to further its strategic goal of the encirclement of both China and of Iran. With Islam-bin Laden at the center of things, all these geo-strategic goals can be occluded, even forgotten.

When the US went to liberate Kuwait in 1990–91, it conducted a massive assault on Iraq to free 2.2 million people, of which only 28 per cent are citizens. Even though justice should not be measured in numbers, one would not be callous to ask why the US went to all this trouble for the al-Sabah family? A fairly straightforward answer was offered by then Vice President George H. Bush (the father of the current president) in 1986. Bush, a Texas oil man like his son, went to Saudi Arabia as oil prices collapsed to tell the oil sheiks about US 'domestic interests and thus the interest of national security'. Oil is a question of US national security, not just because of its vast appetite or addiction to oil (more than fifty per cent of the world's consumption), but also on behalf of the US-based multinationals. Consider that around this time Exxon, Texaco and SoCal (now Unocal) owned a third each of the shares in Saudi oil production, while Gulf and British Petroleum shared the totality of Kuwait's production. US interest in Iraq, today, is about the stability of Gulf oil fields, even as the US talks about democracy, rule of law and the need to overthrow their former ally, Saddam Hussein. In Central Asia, the game is similar, as I shall detail below.

The oil and natural gas lands are currently governed by regimes more invested in commissions and other such forms of corruption, while the populations in these lands are more and more frustrated with their social and economic conditions. The impoverishment of other languages of social protest leads many young people to adopt the garb of Islam to articulate their alienation. The crisis they face is not of Islam, but of a collapse of alternative frameworks, such as pan-Arabism (now perverted by the Ba'ath in Iraq and by the neoliberalism of the Mubarak regime in Egypt) or of socialism (many of whose members earned the gallows from US-backed regimes, such as in Iraq and Egypt, both once home to vibrant communist parties). As the US bombs fell, then, they were not, despite Bush's rhetoric, on a mission against Islam; theirs is a fuel's errand. After rubble had been shifted from one valley of Afghanistan to another, the problem remains – an addiction to oil and natural gas, and the profits it provides the children of the Seven Sisters as opposed to the cultivation of dignity and social well-being in the states that are oil rich. This is the crisis we need to address. This small book, then, is written to explain the record of the US and its neo-feudal allies in their McJihad against the planet, from at least the end of World War II to the present. It does not claim to be comprehensive, nor does it claim to use original research. Rather it summarizes the work of wonderful journalists and scholars who help us put 9/11 and its aftermath in a framework that does justice to all the facts and not just to the prejudices against Islam and for oil.

3

War in Passive Voice

I. UNILATERAL WAR

On October 7, the US–UK bombardment of Afghanistan began. The bombing has begun. Kabul is being bombed. So said the television anchors and the newspapers – all in passive voice, all with an air of inevitability. Finally it is here, said the US population, and we hope it goes away soon. We don't want to be burdened by it, for it may force us to make moral choices that are far too uncomfortable. Better to pretend that it has not happened, or else that its inevitability makes it inconsequential. There is more activity when a storm is on the horizon, when most people rush to the supermarket to buy provisions and to fill their cars with petrol.

Tons of firepower dropped from Herat to Jalalabad – cars lined up from Kabul to Peshawar through the Khyber Pass, like a row of fireflies, unsure if the border will be open or closed. During the entire eighteenth century, one and a half million people crossed the ocean from England to the Americas. In three weeks, about this number of Afghans made their way to a neighbouring country, eager to get out before the bombardment inevitably began. That they left in cars tells us something about their class position. Middle class and elite Afghans left the country in waves, first in the late 1970s to escape the radical egalitarianism of the Marxist regime, then in the 1980s to escape the ravages of the mujahideen assault on the cities, again in the 1990s to escape the radical Islamism of the Taliban and the Northern Alliance, and then in October 2001 to escape the rowdy guns of the US–UK military. By the end of 2001, over five million Afghans joined millions of their brethren in the world of refugees.

Restraint was not the order of the day at the Pentagon or at United States Central Command at MacDill Air Force Base in Florida. Shortly after 9/11, the US Congress authorized $40 billion toward the relief efforts *and* toward the campaign against the perpetrators. Not a week after 9/11, supply ships went on their way from the US toward Diego Garcia in the Indian Ocean, and toward Spain – to prepare the way for an assault that was inevitable. US Defence Secretary Donald Rumsfeld and US Secretary of State Colin Powell travelled to the region and to the neighbours of Afghanistan to forge a 'coalition' against the Taliban, and to see if any of the near-by countries would allow US–UK aircraft and ground troops to use them as forward deployment posts. Opportunism was the name of the game in this period. The rapacious and unscrupulous government of the Hindu Right in India begged for entry into the impatient coalition, pleaded for entry into the oily New World Order without asking for anything for itself except the right to sow terror among Indian Muslims. The Pakistanis came to the table with care, asking for relief on the sanctions due to the nuclear tests, for massive debt relief, and finally for some leverage in its campaign over Kashmir – for this it would be on board the US campaign.

But most of the regional powers declined to proffer unconditional support, except Uzbekistan. Many of the powers had formed relationships during the course of 2001 with the express purpose of removing the Taliban virus from the heart of Asia. In June, the Russians and Chinese joined with Kazakhstan,

Tajikstan and Kyrghyzstan to establish the Shanghai Cooperation Organization (SCO). In its first meeting the SCO passed a resolution in opposition to the US anti-missile plans, to the stern variety of Sunni fundamentalism espoused by the Taliban and funded by the Saudi royals, and to US plans to dominate the sizable oil and natural gas reserves in Central Asia. The Uzbek government later joined this alliance, and it seemed, at the time, that the SCO would undermine the US-sponsored GUUAM (Georgia, Ukraine, Uzbekistan, Azerbaijan and Moldova) group. After the June summit, Kazakh President Nursultan Nazarbaev said, 'the threat facing Central Asia is a threat facing the whole of Eurasia. The source nourishing terrorism and extremism is the instability of Afghanistan'. Afghanistan was at the top of the SCO agenda; the SCO strategically located its counter-terrorism unit in Bishkek (capital of Kyrghyzstan). The process that led to the SCO begins with Iran, a state born out of a radical anti-monarchical revolution that led to the Islamic regime. The Islam of Iran is Shi'ism and it is generally opposed to the types of Sunni fundamentalism that one sees in Saudi Wahabbisim and now among the Taliban, in Chechnya, and elsewhere (bear in mind that the Ayatollahs brought a hierarchical form of Shi'ism to bear on the Iranian population after 1979, and its regime of clerico-fascism degraded the complexity of both everyday Shi'ism and the radical nationalism of Ali Shariati, one of the ideological forebears of the revolution).[1] Interested in an entente against Wahabbi fundamentalism, Iran turned to Russia as early as 1989 (when Khomeni died) to forge an alliance that was given an important push when the Russian foreign minister visited Iran two years ago, and when the reformist President Mohammed Khatami visited Moscow in early 2001. Meanwhile, the Russians and Chinese signed the Good Neighbourly Treaty of Friendship and Cooperation in July 2001 to signal their alliance against US hegemony (especially the missile defence plan). In June 2000, Iran's President Khatami was the first Muslim head of state to visit Kashgar (Xianjiang province, PRC) where he met Islamic scholars at the Grand Mosque (the twelfth century Iranian poet

Sa'adi once said prayers there) and where he indicated his opposition to fundamentalist forms of Islam. This act signalled the seriousness of the regional powers to tackle the scourge of bin Laden-style instability. Iran–China–Russia began to create an anti-imperialist regional compact for Central Asia that could, perhaps, have led to some measure of popular stability in a crisis-prone region.

But it was not to be. Russia, eager to occlude its acts in Chechnya, not only failed to block the war, but Putin eagerly welcomed the US into Central Asia. This is a short-lived alliance as the problems of Central Asian energy reserves and the direction of the pipeline trouble the Putin–Bush camaraderie for the cameras (and Putin, while in Bush's hometown of Crawford, Texas, in early November 2001, refused to budge on the Russian stand against the missile defence project of the US). The story with Iran is complex, and it turns to some extent on the pipeline (a question which we shall deal with below). Eager to sideline Iran for historical and political reasons, Teheran University's Pirouz Mojtahed-Zadeh writes, 'the United States is pursuing such a manifestly anti-Iranian strategy in Caspian-Central Asia regardless of the fact that geography dictates a natural role for Iran in the region'.[2] Khatami's 'dialogue among civilizations' is a non-starter, as Bush followed the fallow Huntington line of a 'clash among civilizations'.

The only regional power to fall in line with the US was Uzbekistan, who had anyway been wary of the SCO (they joined after the June meeting) and who was an active partner of the US military since 1995. Uzbekistan is not an impoverished country; indeed its growth rate has been higher than that of the Baltic states, this mainly because the strong state of President Islam Karimov refused to conduct liberalization or market-oriented IMF-type reforms.[3] On 13 December 1995 the US and Uzbekistan signed an agreement for the US military to train Uzbek troops and to allow the US armed forces access to Central Asian terrain for training. In 1996 the US–Uzbek troops conducted the Balance-Ultra96 exercises in the Ferganskya Valley, a perfect place to train for Afghan warfare. This was followed by other Balance-Ultra trainings, to allow US troops preparations for the terrain and to create close ties with the Uzbek army. In August 1999, Islamic radicals formed the Islamic Movement of Uzbekistan (IMU) whose purpose was to overthrow Karimov's rule and establish a Taliban-type state there (in June 2001 the IMU changed its name to the Islamic Party of Turkestan to signal its intention to create a Taliban state in all of Central Asia). The IMU's leader Tahir Yuldosh tried to assassinate Karimov in February 1999 and in May of that year he obtained permission from the Taliban to create a military training camp and base in northern Afghanistan (in August 2001, the wires reported that Juma Namangami, field commander of the IMU, became one of bin Laden's deputies).[4] Karimov, otherwise a fairly stable authoritarian leader, is under pressure to dispatch the threat from the IMU and an alliance with the US has helped take care of the immediate problems with the IMU camps in northern Afghanistan. Some of this paid off in late November, when Juma Namangami was reported killed by US air strikes.[5]

Uzbekistan's real advantage is this: that there is no democratic press and that Karimov rides roughshod over the Uzbeks means that the US can set up bases that are not only private, but also heavily guarded against terrorist attack (such as the al-Khobar attack in Saudi Arabia). The US tends to favour authoritarian regimes as homes for its bases (Philippines under Marcos being the best example, but also the Prince Sultan Air Base and the Dhahran base in Saudi Arabia); among other reasons, India was sidelined because the government would not have been able to silence the opposition and the press. Pakistan remained an option, among other reasons because of the close ISI–Taliban links, the geographical proximity of Pakistan to Afghanistan, and the need to forge a Pasthu-speaking bloc from Pakistan to ensure that the fight against the Taliban not take on overly ethnic connotations.

II. PAKISTAN'S VISE

Pervez Musharraf, Chief Executive of Pakistan, was in a quandary. In October 1999 he overthrew the venal and corrupt regime of Prime Minister Nawaz Sharif to bring the military back into power after a brief hiatus of bourgeois democracy. But since the constitutional coup of 1954, Pakistan has stumbled with a ruling class keener to aggrandize itself by any means rather than build the productive capacity of the nation toward, perhaps, a future divestment of riches to the people – what we generally call 'development'. Musharraf's act in 1999, then, was not so much a return to dictatorship as perhaps an attempt by a secular, almost Kemalist, wing of the Pakistani military to stave off both the corruptions of the landlord-mercantilist regime and the howls of the theocratic fascists. Political critic Aijaz Ahmad describes Musharraf as a man 'of the more liberal, secular wing: officers of the old stamp. But it may be too late for such as them. There are others, of a different persuasion, waiting in the wings to overwhelm them.'[6] Indeed, the terrorist attacks of 9/11 and the unfolding of the crisis in Afghanistan provided those men in the wings with an opportunity.

President Bush offered the Pakistani government the first ultimatum on the road to war: provide military access to your airspace and your soil or else you will be treated as a state that harbours terrorists. The punishment for that will be swift. Musharraf deliberated, and then conceded. The second ultimatum was to the Taliban and it was a high-level Pakistani team, people from the Inter-Services Intelligence (ISI) that was created, as it happens, during the Afghan wars of the 1980s to harness intelligence from all agencies, but to work in coordination with (but really under the control of) the CIA. General Mahmood Ahmed, head of the ISI, sat with the Taliban at Kandahar and intimated that if bin Laden was not given up, the bombardment would surely begin. The Taliban was clear that it would not act unless the Organization of Muslim States made a formal demand, and if it was shown certain evidence of a link between the WTC and bin Laden. In Pakistan, Foreign Minister Abdul Sattar hoped for a miracle.

It is fitting that the last intermediary to the Taliban came from the Pakistanis. The two other states that had recognized the Taliban regime (Saudi Arabia and the UAE) quickly walked away from their ally, while Pakistan remained till the very end. Pakistan was, after all, the main sponsor of the Taliban, a movement whose origins may be found in the madrassas, those institutions of learning set up in northern Pakistan to impart theological education. The Taliban (literally, students) emerged from these schools under the tutelage of hard-core Islamicists who also produced a slew of activists for the self-styled jihads in Kashmir, Chechnya and elsewhere.

The Pakistanis backed the Taliban for at least three reasons in the war over Afghanistan that began in earnest in the mid-1990s. With the Soviet withdrawal and the collapse of the Marxist regime by 1992, the spoils of Afghanistan lay before the warlords who had been backed to the hilt by the CIA and the Saudi intelligence service, as well as by the Pakistanis. But after 1992, the various warlords held onto sections of the country, being unable to make adjustments with each other, impatiently trapped in a culture of warfare developed during the tussle against the Soviet army. First, the Pakistanis have been nervous about the 1893 Durand Line that divides Pakistan and Afghanistan and divides the Pashtun people into two states. Forced upon the region by the British involvement in the Great Game, the Durand Line was set to expire in 1993; the spectre of Pashtunistan was raised, therefore, for the first time in Pakistan's history.[7] Already laden by secessionist movements in the south and east of the country (and burdened by the loss of East Pakistan in 1971, to become Bangladesh), the Pakistani regime remains sensitive to the problem of the Pashtun population in the north of the country. 'The setting up of the Taliban militia', analyst Maharaj Kaul notes, 'may have, in part, been driven by Pakistan's fear of Pashtun nationalism leading to re-unification with

Afghanistan of the North West Frontier Province which, after 1993, had obtained legal sanctity'.[8] Second, in September 1994 the transport mafia of Pakistan and Afghanistan was eager to secure a route from the former country through the latter into Central Asia. The transport mafia was keen to clear the road from Quetta (Pakistan) to Kandahar (Afghanistan) and then onto Ashakabad (capital of Turkemistan). As the Pakistani Interior Minister Naseerullah Babar negotiated with the warlords, the transport mafia and ISI backed Taliban (in its infancy) captured the border town of Spin Baldak and proved their mettle. From then onward, the transport mafia and the ISI put their faith and funds in the Taliban as the only agent to keep the roads safe for the transit of goods (including opium) in the region. When the Taliban took Kandahar, Babar called them 'our boys', while the transport mafia kept their mouths shut and filled their pockets. This is the second reason for Pakistan's support of the Taliban.[9] The third reason is that the Taliban represents a form of severe Islam that is not alien to the post-Zia Pakistani social world, and this alliance of Wahabbite Islam with the Deobandi Islam of post-Zia Pakistan would guarantee an ally in central Asia who was not pro-India ('we support the jihad in Kashmir', said the Taliban's leader Mullah Omar in 1998).

The Bush administration and the monopoly media evinced great surprise and horror at the Talibanization of Pakistani society, at the groundswell of militant opinion in favour of the Taliban not only in the Pashtun north, but also elsewhere around the country. Such astonishment is unwarranted, as the US well knew of the Talibanization of Pakistan long before the weeks after 9/11, and indeed the government and its policy experts expressed their ambivalent admiration for faith-based, private education in Pakistan. During the battle over the Shariat Bill proposed by then Prime Minister Nawaz Sharif (March 1999), groups such as the Women's Action Forum and the omnibus group Joint Action Committee for People's Rights called the bill a part of the 'Talibanization of Pakistan'. Despite the well-developed critique of Taliban-like policies in Pakistan, in October

2000, US policy analyst and former State Department man Stephen P. Cohen wrote, 'Some madrassas, or religious schools are excellent'. 'Others', he wrote, 'are hotbeds for jihadist and radical Islamic movements', but these, he emphasized, are only about twelve per cent of the total and they 'need to be upgraded to offer their students a modern education'.[10] And why shouldn't Cohen, who was in the news during the Afghan war as an expert on fanaticism and South Asia, write like this? After all, then Presidential candidate G.W. Bush (and Democratic Vice Presidential candidate Joe Lieberman) went on and on about faith-based education, about tax relief to families who want their children to attend private school (what is known, perversely, as 'school choice'). In a sense Pakistan could have shown the US the way since it has already destroyed its secular public institutions in favour of the choice of theocratic fascism. And with the recent fulminations from televangelist Jerry Falwell and Pat Robertson (about how gays and lesbians, civil libertarians and other such symbols of 'promiscuousness' have forced God to turn his back on the US, and send 9/11 as a wake-up call), we can be sure that faith-based schools and charity promise to Talibanize the United States as well.

And again, like so much else, the destruction of Pakistani education is not just the fault of a corrupt and unprincipled ruling elite. It bears within it at least two other forces. The first agent of change in Pakistan has been the visible hand of the International Monetary Fund. Pakistan is cotton country, with two thirds of its exports tied to this sector, but most of it is low-value added unprocessed cotton or low-count yarn that is sent off to the advanced industrial states for a nineteenth century style turn around – export cheap raw materials, import expensive finished products. In 1993, Pakistan, abandoned by a general global decline in the profit margins from cotton, turned to the IMF for aid and initiated the Structural Adjustment Policy (SAP) that has now become legendary around the world. A month before the coup of 1999, Nawaz Sharif's finance minister Ishaq Dar told the press that 'the government has done everything possible. We have provided the conducive environment' for foreign investors.[11] Aggressive acts of neoliberalism became the hallmark of the regime. 'Distortions', such as public institutions, came under attack from the IMF and Pakistan's already weak education sector came under fiscal pressure. A weak educational infrastructure moved much of the lower middle class toward private education in the low to moderate cost madrassas. The IMF, then, helped move many of Pakistan's youth to religion.

A second agent of the madness is the Cold War, and Pakistan's efforts to gain international strength by linkages with Europe–US. On 24 February 1955, only a few months since President Ghulam Mohammed disbanded the constitutional government (28 October 1954), Pakistan joined those other votaries of the 'free world' in the Baghdad Pact: places such as the Kingdom of Iraq, the United Kingdom, the Kingdom of Iran and the Republic of Turkey. Five years later, Pakistan tied its hands to the United States in the Central Treaty Organization (CENTO), a US-run alliance of states in west Asia. But for several decades the US did not provide the kind of support expected by Pakistan, so much so that at a CENTO conference on 30 April 1963, then foreign minister Zulfikar Ali Bhutto attacked the United States' aid policies to India as opposed to its indifference toward Pakistan.

It was only with the Iranian revolution and the establishment of the Ayatollahs to power, as well as with the Soviet entry into Afghanistan, both in 1979, that Pakistan became important to the United States. All those years of waiting paid off for the ruling class, because for a brief instant, during the 1980s, the US seemed to be in the country to stay. Giddy with expectation, the Pakistani elite welcomed the transformation of the society, created the ISI for the CIA's use in Afghanistan, and then pushed ahead all manner of neoliberal cruelties on an already impoverished nation. Certainly the per capita income increased during these years, but class inequality widened beyond imagination. From 1982 to 1992, Pakistan's population grew by a third while basic infrastructural services (water, sewage, electricity, housing, education, health facilities) only grew by 6.9 per cent. Even those at the World Bank who collect these statistics became horrified.

By the time Afghanistan crumbled into the hands of the Taliban in 1996, Pakistan had already been abandoned by the US, like a tired warhorse sent off to pasture without so much as a bag of oats. Congress stopped the sale of F-16 aircraft even after Pakistani hard currency had changed hands; sanctions for this or that plagued the US-Pakistan relationship, as the US tried to disentangle from its ally and reach out to the emergent market of one billion Indians. In 1995, slow GDP growth and high inflation forced the Pakistani government to curtail the IMF programmes, thereby losing loans and other revenue supports. The government turned on its people again, this time with a devaluation of the rupee by seven per cent (this over and above a three per cent gradual depreciation), a seven per cent increase in oil prices and the imposition of a five to ten per cent regulatory duty on imports, as well as a tighter monetary policy. The macro indicators smiled, and so did the IMF, but the mass of the population entered an economic sinkhole.

No wonder, then, that US-style capitalism seems so remote and unreasonable, because while the dollar elite make good in the cities, the rupee masses seem to run up against the walls of the local madrassa. In 1995, the year of the downfall, UNESCO reported that almost two thirds of the adults in Pakistan are illiterate, and of women, the number rises to three quarters. The working class and peasantry do not have access to any education, and the vibrant free press in Pakistan (it has been so since 1987, although there are always attempts to curtail it) has produced excellent work on the disenfranchisement of this vast section of humanity. The dollar elite holds a monopoly to the finest schools and colleges, and many of them find their way to colleges in Europe–US since the profits of the mercantilist–landlord set-up enable them to pay full freight. The lower middle class and whatever exists of the middle class does not have access to either decent public education or to the English-medium private schools. They go to the madrassas.

'As Pakistan's state-run educational system steadily collapsed', writes Pakistani journalist Ahmed Rashid, 'these madrassas became the only avenue for boys from poor families to receive the semblance of an education.'[12] By the late 1980s, the madrassas already numbered over thirty thousand (with about a third of them registered with the government), and most of them existed even then along Pakistan's border with Afghanistan. These madrassas claim their lineage from the 1860s when an Islamic seminary was formed in Deoband (northern India), a lineage that is textually conservative and, in its current incarnations, as orthodox as Saudi Wahhabism. The Deobandis filled the interstices of Pakistani society, notably in the sphere of education, and their political agencies turned their attention more to armed rebellion than to electoral politics. While the Jama'at-i-Ulema-i-Islam, the political wing of the Deobandis (whose main arm is the Jama'at-i-Islami), drew a virtual blank in the otherwise boycotted elections of 1985, the same formation mobilizes over two hundred thousand cadres to its annual conventions (latterly close to half a million people come to its conferences). The Lashkar-e-Toiba, perhaps the most orthodox of the right and one that only draws three per cent of its followers from the madrassas, calls upon four hundred thousand to its annual conventions at its home base in Muridke. This power translated into political capital in 1993 when Benazir Bhutto welcomed Jama'at cadre into her government. Elections, therefore, are of no interest to the Jama'at when it already controls the base of Pakistani society.

What seems to bother many people is that the terrorists of 9/11 were older and better educated than one expects. But this should not be a surprise because the madrassas attract the lower middle to middle class, mainly boys with poor prospects of class advancement or even of class maintenance. The Jama'at and the generally liberal Tehrik Minhaj-ul-Quran draw from this class set, while the Tanzeem-ul-Ikhwan, according to writer Arif Jamal, appeals to retired army officers who retreat into the world of the middle class.[13] Not only, therefore, are key people in the army part of these formations, but many analysts make the case that the rank and file and junior officers took their own education in the madrassas alongside those who became professional jehadis and it is this lot that did not take Musharraf's concessions to the US and against the Taliban easily. The madrassas have close ties with the Taliban as well as the rank and file of the Pakistani army, and any resentment against US-driven globalization that one has, the other shares. This continues to be Musharraf's quandary.

To put Kashmir on the agenda as a bargaining chip was perhaps a way to mollify the rank and file, and avert a certain coup as the aerial bombardment began. Without a doubt the permanent military presence of the US in the region produces a 'domino effect' of instability that plays into the hands of the right-wing forces across the subcontinent. The Fifth Afghan War breeds further instability in South Asia and leaves intact a volatile mix of social forces: the possibility of a coup against Musharraf and his Kemalist officer clique in Pakistan (this unless the US throws a massive amount of money into Pakistan to buy off the impoverished – an unlikely proposition given the start of an official recession in the buyer of last resort; or unless Musharraf takes the al-Sadat route in Egypt to create an immense machinery to oppress an unhappy population); a momentarily defeated, but ideologically hardened Taliban-like network in Central Asia; a retreat of those who foment terror in Kashmir from their bases in southern Afghanistan and into either Pakistan proper or Pakistani Occupied Kashmir; and meanwhile in India, the strengthened hand of the coalition government led by the BJP, the mirror image of the Jama'at. All these theocratic regimes have at least one thing in common: they have slammed the brakes on the dialectics of history. The answer offered by many of these forces to the woes of capitalism is (as among the Jama'at in Pakistan and the radical Islamists in Central Asia) 'Islamic economics' or (as among the Swadeshi Jagran Manch) 'Hindu economics', a combination of neoclassical capitulation to 'market forces' sugar-coated with words like *zakat*, but without a coherent programme for the revitalization of social life. Unwilling to see the contradictions of social life in the modern world, most of them, like the US President, tend to divide the world into Good and Evil, in stark moral categories that fail to capture the mess of human life. If those whom you disagree with are Evil, then nothing remains for you to do than to kill them.

III. THE INDULGENCES OF HINDUTVA

South of the war, in India, the Hindu Right was gleeful.

Right after 9/11, the Prime Minister Atal Bihari Vajpayee, considered a moderate in his party, but nevertheless far right of reason, sent off a letter to President Bush to mark the condolences of the Indian people. But further, he pointed out like the Israeli government, that India has lived with terror for some time now, and that terror, he intimated, has an Islamic face.

The message was set: India has lived with terrorism for years, and the government and military would be ready to put any means at the disposal of the US government and military to thwart it. Vajpayee sent his External Affairs and Defence Minster, Jaswant Singh, to meet with the Bush administration on 1–2 October 2001, but also to turn over two urns to New York City's Mayor Rudy Guiliani. The urns, one with waters from nine of India's rivers, and the other with the soil of India, are to be interned in the memorial to the fallen. Mr. Singh continued Vajpayee's message with a string of banal words: 'India's commitment to values that we share with the United States of America to democracy, to free speech, to freedom of individuals to a certain way of life, of which terrorism is the very antithesis, and our commitment to stand shoulder to shoulder with the United States of America for these values, in this fight against terrorism, is in no fashion less than anyone else's'.

Not two decades ago, no major Indian leader promised such fealty, indeed most Indian leaders, even the pro-US Rajiv Gandhi, tried to maintain some distance from the State Department and the Pentagon. US interests in South Asia rarely matched those of the Indian state, and furthermore, most Indian leaders recognized that the canard of democracy did not do justice to the truth of US foreign policy. The US, for almost four decades, preferred to sit with the Pakistani generals than with the incomplete democracy of India. Things have now changed, even as Musharraf sits on a tightrope stretched out by the Bush administration, the Hindu Right hopes to ingratiate itself with the powers that be.

The military centrality of Pakistan to this assault meant that India, once again, was to be relegated to the sidelines of the US war and diplomatic plans. But the Hindu Right-dominated government was nonplussed. It almost immediately banned the Students Islamic Movement of India (SIMI), a group formed in 1977 to represent the abysmal educational opportunities for Muslim youth in India, but which has in an environment poisoned by Hindutva supremacy, turned to an outrageous sectarianism of its own. It arrested six students from a socialist group in eastern Delhi as they distributed pamphlets against the war – the charges amount to sedition, not against India, but against the US! It invoked the spectre of Islamic terrorism within India to scare the people of Uttar Pradesh to vote for Hindutva at all costs in the February 2002 state elections. And much of the latter was accomplished by the flourish of a single date: 12 May 1993.

On 12 May 1993 explosions rocked the city of Mumbai and over two hundred people died. These Mumbai blasts are the symbol now of India's 9/11, of India's claim to being a victim of terrorism. But what are the Mumbai blasts and are they *sui generis*? By all indications the underworld of criminals, movie financiers and Dubai-based businessmen set explosives in several buildings in Mumbai as a ghastly and senseless retaliation for the Hindutva engineered massacre of Muslims and others during the Mumbai riots of December 1992–January 1993, an event that shattered Mumbai's cosmopolitanism.

A look at the Srikrishna Commission documents and at the three volumes of documentation turned in by the government of Maharashtra to the Justice Liberhan Commission (and studied ably by Praveen Swami and Anupama Katakam in *Frontline* magazine[14]) makes it clear that the organized Hindu Right bears responsibility for the riots and, crucially, should be found guilty of premeditated violence. There was nothing spontaneous about this riot, and even the word 'riot' does the organized violence an injustice. Intelligence officials collected data on Hindutva's armed brigands ('some of the activists are likely to carry lathis and daggers') and noted that all anti-Muslim sectarian activity 'should be nipped in the bud'. Nothing was done because a senior official felt that these are 'purely religious activities'.

'For five days in December 1992 (December 6 to 10) and fifteen days in January 1993 (January 6 to 20), Bombay, prima urbs of this country, was rocked by riots and violence unprecedented in magnitude and ferocity, as though the forces of Satan were let loose, destroying human values and civilised behaviour': so wrote the High Court Justice B.N. Srikrishna at the start of his official report on the massacre (delivered on 16 February 1998, and already gathering dust).[15] The report, for all its flaws, shows us that the riots came as a result of Hindutva's demolition of the historical mosque at Ayodhya in northern India and as a result of an emboldened Hindutva activist base wanting to participate in some way in that insult to Indian Muslims. 'From January 9, 1993, at least', the Srikrishna Commission reports, 'there is no doubt that the Shiv Sena and Shiva Sainiks took the lead in organising the attacks on Muslims and their properties under the guidance of several leaders of the Shiv Sena . . . Mr. Bal Thackery, who, like a veteran General, commanded his loyal Shiv Sainiks to retaliate by organized attacks against Muslims'. If you doubt the pogrom, the report shows us that of the nine hundred or so killed in the riots, five hundred and seventy five (or almost two-thirds) were Muslims. For the past fifteen years, at least, Indian civil society has taken a beating from these very theocratic organizations, now in power in India. The Hindu Right, as well as the gerontocratic Congress Party, has engineered anti-Muslim and anti-oppressed caste riots, as well as marginalized all those who do not fit into its narrow mould of Indianness.

Two days after the outrageous blasts of May, Home Minister, L.K. Advani denied that the RDX blasts had any connection to the engineered pogrom. Tragedy brings forth its own kind of political amnesia. And now, the Hindu Right brings up May 1993 without any consideration of January 1993, simply to show its fealty to the US in what it sees as a war against Islamic terrorism, whether in Kashmir or elsewhere.

All this would have been inconceivable prior to 1991, when the Indian government (then run by the tired Congress party) turned to a full-fledged neoliberal agenda. The US, under Clinton, sensed that the size of the Indian market (as large as the population of France, salivated Lloyd Bentsen, Clinton's first Treasury Secretary: 'within India lies an upper middle class economy the size of France, and the challenge is to unlock that potential and spread that prosperity', October 1993). An immediate impact of neoliberalism for India was that thousands of workers won their pink slips of unemployment in 1992–93 and many more joined them the following year. The 'potential' is in the profits, not in the well-being of the population. Clinton's visit to India, the military links between the Indian and US army, the tie-ins with Israel, the further 'liberalization' of the economy, the creation of the Bill Gates (Seattle)–Chandrababu Naidu (Hyderabad) virtual axis, the employment of External Affairs Minister Jaswant Singh as practically a mouthpiece for the US State Department, the anti-China rhetoric of the Hindu Right and the nuclear tests to ensure that the US has a second front against China – all this amounts to the catalogue of India–US relations, a marked change from the Nehruvian Third Way.

But the rate of return for servility is very low. India's economy remains in the doldrums (with an increase in inequality with each budget), its military has not been invited to be the junior partner in Afghanistan (indeed it seems likely that, for the near future, Pakistan will come back in US favour – if Musharraf survives), the Kashmir question will not be solved as per Hindutva's specifications, and furthermore the collapse of the Nasdaq and of the tech-world means that one of India's new exports (IT workers and software) may also be hit (even as it currently appears to be beneath the radar of the international decline in the profits of the information sector).

In its negotiations with the US, it seems that Islamabad was able to extract some support from Washington for its position regarding Kashmir. New Delhi, unable to win the hearts and minds of the Kashmiri people, has pledged itself to a US-brokered settlement, one that does not bode well for the Kashmiri people if the experience of Bosnia and Palestine is to be kept in mind. The current crisis in Kashmir is not ageless, nor should its roots be taken back to 1948 or to the UN resolutions about it. The present problems stem from the economic and political devastation that followed the death of Sheikh Mohammed Abdullah on 8 September 1982, an incident that put into disarray the mild form of stability constituted by the skill of the Sheikh and the relatively careful governance from New Delhi. Kashmir's present history, since then, is in four phases: 1983–88, marked by the political venality both of Indira Gandhi's Congress and Farooq Abdullah's National Conference; 1988–91, characterized by the upsurge of young Kashmiris for '*azaadi*' manifested in the Jammu and Kashmir Liberation Front; 1991–93, distinguished by Pakistan's usurpation of the revolt through the offices of the Hizbul Mujahideen and other Pakistani-*pasand* organizations; finally, the current phase, in which a proxy war continues between ISI-trained and supported *mehmeen* mujahideen (foreign, mainly Afghani Arab type mercenaries) and the Indian forces whose interlude was the Kargil war of 1999.[16]

The Pakistani military did send a rag-tag bunch of fighters into Kashmir in 1948 and 1965, but by the late 1980s the ISI's deployments had a different cast. 'Steeled by the Afghan war', wrote journalist Manoj Joshi, the ISI systematically planned for action in Kashmir from 1984. It trained those opposed to India and allowed the insurgency 'in Kashmir to ripen so that the fruit would fall of its own accord into Pakistani laps'.[17] In February 1990, Gulbuddin Hikmatyar, the Afghan militant, told a crowd at Peshawar that India in Kashmir might face the same fate as the Soviets in his native land. The confidence of the Afghan campaign provided the ISI with personnel and prestige for their Kashmir intrigues. Simultaneously, the rise of the Hindu Right in India alienated many Kashmiri Muslims from what some militants, following Jamaat founder Maulana Maudoodi, called the 'theodemocracy' of India.[18] The VHP's *shilanyas* campaign of 1989, L.K. Advani's Rath Yatra of 1991, Murli Mahohar Joshi's Ekta Yatra of late 1991, and the demolition of the Babri Masjid of 1992 all contributed to the growth of militancy in Kashmir. Joshi's Ekta Yatra concluded in Srinagar and its great contribution was toward the unity (*ekta*) of the militants in the valley. The strengthened resolve of the militants provided the ISI with a vast opening for their infiltrators. The shenanigans of the Sangh (or Jang) *parivar* and the ruthlessness of the ISI came together to foment Kashmir's current woes.

The Kashmiri people have a right to descry the onset of violence against them, both from the ISI backed organizations and from an Indian army now without a legitimate political rudder. New Delhi is correct to point to terror that is husbanded in Pakistan, which was trained in Afghanistan and then sent across the border to create mayhem in Kashmir. ISI Chief General Akhtar Abdul Rehman was eager to export the ISI's Afghan-style guerrilla warfare into the valley in the late 1980s and the ISI did so by systematically sidelining the Jammu and Kashmir Liberation Front and by promoting the Hizbul Mujahideen. In 1987, near Lahore, the ISI and Saudi money founded the Markaz Dawa-ul-Irshad and its military wing, the Lashkar-e-Toiba. Founded by university teachers (again like the Taliban), the Markaz is linked to the Jama'at-ul-Ulema Islam (the pro-Taliban faction led by Maulana Fazlur Rahman, famous for wielding a gun at political rallies). The Lashkar now dominates much of the militancy in the valley, in much the same was as the Pakistani-backed 'Afghan Arabs' took their place beside the Taliban. But the nub of the matter is that such groups would not gain a foothold unless the practices of the Indian state had also failed them. To blame an insurgency on 'foreign' groups is to miss the depth of suffering engendered by the state through a lack of imaginative economic planning and social development. In the last decade, over twenty thousand people have died in Kashmir as a result of the conflict, and a vast number have been affected in myriad ways. The gun has become the arbiter of political differences, and it was the guns of the Hizbul Mujahideen which made the Jama'at a political force. The Indian army responds with guns and with torture, as New Delhi washes its hands off a political solution. In all this, the sage words of Nehru are often forgotten: 'People seem to forget that Kashmir is not a commodity for sale or to be bartered. It has an individual existence and its people must be the final arbiters of their future' (6 July 1951).

The indulgence of Hindutva is not to find a genuine solution that befits the people of Kashmir, for it uses Kashmir and the violence there as a means to curry favour with the US in its obsession with the War on Terrorism. 'Swadeshi' foreign policy is not inclined toward solutions because its reason, driven by its own astrological forecasts, is this: to make Islam the global enemy and to wait for the day when Delhi–Tel Aviv–Washington (and London, somewhere on the axis) becomes the new global cities that count. These cities, the Hindu Right hopes, will be the centerpieces of the Communities of Democracy envisaged by Madeleine Albright, the harbingers of US-driven free market policies the world over; and, like any good middleman, Hindutva hopes to get a few per cent cut on the global takings. The indulgence of Hindutva–Zionism–Manifest Destinyism is this: 9/11 forgives their own acts of commission and allows them freehand to produce the world in their image.

IV. A DIGRESSION ON AERIAL BOMBARDMENT

Everything is predictable. The way the alliances would be forged, the eagerness of the Hindu Right and of Islam Karimov, the vise of Musharraf, the quiet but unflinching accommodation of the Saudi regime, the collaborationist stance from Russia, the critical noises from Iran, the cautious silence from the PRC.

The aerial sorties, the helicopter operations, the Special Forces raids, the encouragement of a local ally (here the Northern Alliance) – much of it was laid out at the Berlin Track 2 meeting, but most of it is Gulf War redux. What was also predictable was the inevitable 'errant cluster bomb' and the 'collateral damage'.

Reports came in almost immediately from sources that the US tends to consider 'unconfirmed' (such as Iranian television and the Al-Jazeera network) that 'errant bombs' landed in civilian areas and took civilian lives. We heard of the bombs on a UN mine-removal office in Kabul, we heard of the two strikes on Herat, and we heard about the bombing of the CNN in Kandahar as well as the Al-Jazeera network office. *The New York Times* reported 'the Pentagon has said errors were unavoidable in a bombing campaign of the intensity of that being conducted in Afghanistan'.[19] The United Nations, whose credibility is stretched to the limit once again, reports that 'residential areas and some villages' have become targets of 'errant cluster bombs' because 'Taliban troops have moved into those areas'. In the first few days of December, the US bombed the region of Tora Bora in search of bin Laden and about two thousand al-Qa'ida fighters, but on both occasions the bombs fell on Northern Alliance troops and civilians. In the first raid, Hazarat Ali, the law and order minister for the Eastern Shura told the press that seventy people had died, and that he had been in touch with US command; 'we told them, "Your bombing is not on the mark. There are civilians there. Stop bombing that area".' In Tampa, Florida, at Central Command, Rear Admiral Craig R. Quigley said, 'there was no chance the village was targeted improperly'.[20] The next day, around Agam just south of Jalalabad, another one hundred people died due to the air strikes. This time the US press officer in Islamabad noted that the air force was 'investigating' the attack on the village and a Northern Alliance office.[21] There is little concern that however smart we think the bombs can be, 'errors' in the world of aerial bombardment are inevitable.

To say that the civilian deaths from aerial bombardment are

unintentional is sophistry, because if there is a probability that the bombs will hit civilian targets, then *ipso facto* the civilian deaths are not unintentional. This is tantamount to saying that a drunk driver who did not intend to kill someone in an 'accident' should be set free for good motives; US law prosecutes drunk drivers regardless of whether they have been in an accident, because it recognizes that drunk driving is an inevitable accident. The same must be said of aerial bombardment. It always already *intends* to kill civilians, despite the best intentions of the military planners.

Early laws on warfare recognized the question of 'intention' as sophistry, but even here there was a desire to accommodate flagrant acts of military violence. It began well in 1899 and then went downhill by 1907. Hague II (Laws and Customs of War on Land, 29 July 1899; and ratified by the US Senate on 14 March 1902) was farsighted in its insistence (article XXIII) that military combat should prohibit 'arms, projectiles, or material of a nature to cause superfluous injury'. By Hague IV (18 October 1907, and ratified by the US Senate the next year) the last phrase was amended to read, 'to cause unnecessary suffering'.

But all this was before the present history of bombing.[22] For the first act of aerial bombardment only took place on 26 October 1911 when the Italian air force bombed Tripoli in their war against Turkish North Africa. As a reaction to the violent turn of air warfare and the fear that it would be turned against each other, the powers committed to end aerial bombardment, but the treaty they penned did not come into effect. That rather farsighted treaty (Draft Rules on Aerial Warfare, February 1923) pointedly noted (in article XXII) that 'aerial bombardment for the purpose of terrorizing the civilian population, of destroying or damaging private property not of military character, or of injuring non-combatants is prohibited', and furthermore (according to article XXIV) any belligerent state that did bomb civilian targets had to compensate them.

The very next year Squadron Leader Arthur 'Bomber' Harris of the Royal Air Force ruthlessly bombed the Kurds and Iraqis.

In March of 1924, Harris reported the following to his superiors (the text of which was added to the RAF's August 1924 'Notes on the Method of Employment of Air Arm in Iraq', a report to Parliament, thereafter expunged from the record): 'Where the Arab and Kurd had just begun to realize that if they could stand a little noise they could stand bombing . . . they now know what real bombing means, in casualties and damage; they now know that within forty-five minutes a full-sized village (vide attached photos of Kushan-Al-Ajaza) can be practically wiped out and a third of its inhabitants killed or injured by four or five machines which offer them no real target, no opportunity for glory as warriors, no effective means of escape'.[23]

By the time the next major convention against aerial bombing was drafted, all the major powers joined in the immorality of bombardment. The Spanish in Morocco, over the city of Chechaouen; the French in Syria (the bombardment of Damascus' neighbourhoods on 18 October 1925); the United States in Central America (the bombardment of revolutionary Nicaraguan farmers in the 1920s); and finally, those who started it, the Italians in Ethiopia in 1935–36. As Lindquist puts it, 'the truth about Chechaouen required no cover-up. Bombing natives was considered quite natural. The Italians did it in Libya, the French did it in Morocco, and the British did it throughout the Middle East, in India, and East Africa, while the South Africans did it in Southwest Africa. Will any ambassador ever ask for forgiveness for that? Of all these bombed cities and villages, only Guernica [in Spain, bombed by the Fascists in 1937] went down in history. Because Guernica lies in Europe. In Guernica, *we* were the ones who died.'[24]

On the eve of World War II, on 30 September 1938, the League of Nations produced a unanimous resolution entitled 'Protection of Civilian Populations Against Bombing from the Air in Case of War'. The League declared, 'Intentional bombing of civilian populations is illegal' mainly because 'on numerous occasions public opinion has expressed through the most authoritative channels its horror of the bombing of civilian populations'. The key word here is 'intentional' and the League did not go over the philosophical conundrums posed by the word, as they perhaps should have to prevent the sophistry of 'collateral damage' and 'errant cluster bombs'. On the first day of World War II (1 September 1939), US President Franklin D. Roosevelt wrote a note to the governments of France, Germany, Italy, Poland and the United Kingdom, begging them to desist from aerial bombardment. The note bears quotation in full: 'The ruthless bombing from the air of civilians in unfortified centres of population during the course of the hostilities which have raged in various quarters of the earth during the past few years, which has resulted in the maiming and in the death of thousands of defenseless men, women, and children, has sickened the hearts of every civilized man and woman, and has profoundly shocked the conscience of humanity. If resort is had to this form of inhuman barbarism during the period of the tragic conflagration with which the world is now confronted, hundreds of thousands of innocent human beings who have no responsibility for, and who are not even remotely participating in, the hostilities which have now broken out, will lose their lives. I am therefore addressing this urgent appeal to every government which may be engaged in hostilities publicly to affirm its determination that its armed forces shall in no event, and under no circumstances, undertake the bombardment from the air of civilian populations or of unfortified cities, upon the understanding that these same rules of warfare will be scrupulously observed by all of their opponents. I request an immediate reply.'

The immediate reply was on 20 June 1940 when the Royal Air Force began the bombardment of Germany (and declared that industrial centers and the workers' homes beside them are legitimate targets), and when the Nazi regime began the Blitz against the British on 6 September. Munich, Coventry, London, Hamburg, and then finally Dresden – this was the barbarism of aerial bombardment within Europe. On 27 July 1943, the RAF killed 50,000 people in Hamburg. Reflecting on this barbarity, nuclear physicist Freeman Dyson who was then a clerk for Arthur

'Bomber' Harris wrote that the Nazis 'had sat in their offices, writing memoranda and calculating how to murder people efficiently, just like me. The main difference was that they were sent to jail or hanged as war criminals, while I went free'.[25] Eighty per cent of all the bombs in World War II fell in the last ten months of the war during which the British, for instance, decided to bomb residential areas with the argument that this would foreshorten the war. The US borrowed this logic at Hiroshima and Nagasaki, but only after the USAF firebombed Tokyo on 8 May (General Curtis LeMay who directed the operations, said 'we knew we were going to kill a lot of women and kids when we burned that town. Had to be done').[26] On 13 February 1945, the RAF killed 100,000 in Dresden; on 6 August 1945, the USAF killed 100,000 instantly in Hiroshima (another 100,000 died over the course of the next year). Two days later, the Soviets, the British, the French and the US signed the Nuremberg principles – an act of utter hypocrisy. A 'war crime' (article VI) is specifically defined by these principles as the 'wanton destruction of cities, towns or villages, or devastation not justified by military necessity'. No action was taken against the signatories, now the guardians of the new world order.

Not even against the French army in Madagascar, where the French massacred by bombardment 89,000 to 100,000 people in 1948 in the anti-colonial wars. Nor was there to be any action against the US Air Force for its acts in Korea (1950–53). A senior officer in General MacArthur's command hoped that a harsh US attack would 'give these yellow bastards what is coming to them'. The racist hatred of the Asians took the form of ruthless destruction, such as aerial raids on the northern part of the peninsula to destroy irrigation dams that provided water for three-quarters of the north's food production. 'The subsequent flash flood waters wiped out [supply routes, etc]', the US Air Force noted in an official report. 'The Westerner can little conceive the awesome meaning which the loss of [rice] has for the Asian – starvation and slow death'.[27] From Korea to Vietnam, to the carpet bombardment of Cambodia . . . the list is endless from here on, and Lindquist covers some of the ground for us. The US dropped four times the amount of firepower on Vietnam than was used in the entire Second World War, a tonnage equivalent to six hundred and forty Hiroshimas – some of this includes the 373,000 tons of napalm that seared the Vietnamese landscape and made the construction of socialism in that land so much harder.

In 1964, US President Lyndon Johnson built on the fabricated Tonkin Gulf incident to demand that the military be allowed to employ 'all necessary measures' in the war. Since then we have moved to depleted uranium, to talk of tactical nuclear missiles, and the routine use of napalm and cruise missiles. On 19 December 1968, the UN's 'Resolution on Human Rights' affirmed the International Red Cross's 1965 Vienna statement that combatants cannot adopt 'unlimited' means to injure the enemy, that 'it is prohibited to launch attacks against the civilian populations' and (here we are on weak territory that dilutes the problem of the 'intentional') 'that the distinction must be made at all times between persons taking part in the hostilities and members of the civilian population to the effect that the latter be spared as much as possible'. *As much as possible* – not entirely, not totally. There will be casualties – this is the *realism*, the *pragmatism* of the racist contemporary – where we accept as given that a few of the dehumanized other will succumb to the pedagogy of the bomb despite our best, most civilized intentions.

In 1996 the International Court of Justice, bombarded with three million signatures on an anti-nuclear petition, among other incentives, voted 'unanimously, that threat or use of nuclear weapons is illegal' when it violates various UN statutes, but three justices (from Sierra Leone, Guyana and Sri Lanka) wanted to go further and ban nuclear weapons under any circumstances. They knew that bombs such as these are used basically against those of colour, those who are already subhuman to Europe–US, seen to require the rod for discipline, seen to be a civilization apart. Lindquist documents the genocidal fantasies of Europe–

US against the coloured Other, from Charles Dilke's 1869 *Greater Britain* (which calls for the 'gradual extinction of the inferior races' as a 'blessing of mankind' and does so as airplanes drop 'a rain of awful death to every breathing thing [in China], a rain that exterminates the hopeless race') to Jack London's 1910 *The Unparalled Invasion* (which calls for an aerial bombardment of the Chinese by fragile glass tubes that carry every possible biological weapon – and those that flee are felled by the powers at their borders, the land is disinfected and then whites move into a cleansed China). 'The dream of solving all the problems of the world through mass destruction from the air was already in place', Lindquist writes, 'before the first bomb was dropped'.[28]

Right through the war we heard that the US may use tactical nuclear devices, and we will soon find out that the US did use depleted uranium shells (as they did in Yugoslavia and in Iraq). The US has used cluster munitions, bombs such as the CBU-103s that releases about two hundred BLU-97 bomblets over a wide area. BLU-97 has a high initial failure rate, which means that tens of thousands of these bombs, according to an estimate done in late November by Human Rights Watch, lie unexploded across the Afghan landscape. The unexploded BLU-97 bomblets come in yellow packets, and on 1 November the US military acknowledged that the colour of the packets resembles that of the casing around the food packets. The bombs, said HRW's senior armaments researcher Mark Hiznay, 'pose an extreme hazard to civilians, not just now but for years to come'.[29] The Pakistani government sealed its borders during much of the conflict and sent back refugees to their desolation. The UN High Commissioner on Refugees, Mary Robinson, called for an end to the bombardment so that food could be sent into Afghanistan, real food not the measly food drops orchestrated for propaganda by the US State Department. None of this was to be heeded, as the campaign continued, as bombs fell, as 'errant cluster bombs' landed on civilian targets who became 'collateral damage'. The Taliban bombed without concern for human life, Hikmatyar (a great CIA asset) once killed 25,000 people by indiscriminate rocket fire into Kabul, and now the US bombed 'with precision' from the air, to devastate the productive capacity of Afghanistan and leave it as easy pickings for the next marauder who wants a strategic post on the Great Silk Road. There are those who die 'unintentionally' and then there will be those who will starve because aerial bombing has decapitated the capacity of the country.

V. WAR AIMS

The US State Department–Pentagon has a bad record on war aims. During the lead-up to the Gulf War, the Bush administration, Part 1, argued that the US was needed to liberate Kuwait. The invasion of a state of 2.2 million people, in which only 28 per cent earned the right to citizenship and a part of the oil wealth, was to be liberated by the full force of the US military. The number of ships and aircraft that went toward the Gulf revealed that the size of the deployment was far greater than needed to dispatch the Iraqi army from Kuwait. Something else was on the mind of the State Department. Indeed, the war aims of Bush I transmuted from the liberation of Kuwait to the overthrow of the Ba'athist regime led by Saddam Hussein from Iraq. Even as he addressed the nation two hours after US planes unloaded their payloads on the Iraqi people, Bush I did not talk of the removal of Hussein from power. 'We are determined to knock out Saddam Hussein's nuclear bomb potential', he said on 16 January 1991. 'We will destroy his chemical weapons facilities. Much of Saddam's artillery and tanks will be destroyed'. On 26 February, the Iraqi forces left Kuwait; on 6 March, Bush I told Congress that 'the war in Iraq is over'; by 7 April the Alliance established the northern no-fly zone and began the intermittent bombardment of Iraq (and the major bombing of December 1998), in effect continuing the war till this day. The war aim now is the overthrow of Saddam Hussein, and indeed there continues to be talk that once the Afghan war comes to a close, the US armed forces may attempt another assault to topple

Saddam Hussein. Indeed, as 2001 comes to a close, we have begun to hear about a Phase 2 of the 'War Against Terrorism': a massive assault on Iraq, plus campaigns perhaps against Somalia, Sudan, Lebanon, Indonesia and the Philippines. In the last two archipelagoes, we hear that the governments of these two states are in touch with the US military and are eager to join with them in military assaults on radical Islamist bases on remote islands.

The war aims in retaliation to 9/11 transmuted faster than they did in 1991, but in a most expected fashion. With no firm proof, and reminiscent of the 1995 Oklahoma City bombing,[30] the Bush administration, Part 2, put its finger on Osama bin Laden. In 1998, the Clinton administration bombed Sudan and Afghanistan without warning for the bombings at the eastern African embassies by a network that may be linked directly to bin Laden. This time, Bush II was interested in a comprehensive solution and not a symbolic bombardment. 'Infinite Justice' was the first name of the campaign (since renamed to 'Enduring Peace' after criticism from the oil sheikhs who said that only the divinity can be infinitely just). Musharraf agreed to join the alliance to bring bin Laden to trial, but not to threaten the Taliban regime in Afghanistan. After all, the Taliban are an old Pakistani ally and Pakistan was then only one of three countries to recognize their rule. Within days it became apparent that the war aims had shifted: the US government was not to be content with bin Laden, but it wanted the demise of the Taliban.

To replace the Taliban, the US and the UN sought out several options, including a power sharing agreement between the deposed king, Zahir Shah, and the Northern Alliance, as well as some Pashtun groups from the south (and perhaps 'moderate' Taliban commanders). Zahir Shah has lived in Rome since 1973, and he has over the years, most recently in November 1999, tried to convene a Loya Jirga, or an elders meeting, which would include the brigands who remain locked out of Kabul. Shah, a pensioner of an unnamed Gulf State, is apparently an unwilling protagonist, but those who have funded him for three decades are perhaps eager to see him back in power – to give them title to the Turkmenistan–Pakistan natural gas pipeline. Just as the US joined hands with and funded the unpleasant Iraqi National Congress, the Trojan horse for US imperialism in this case will be the Northern Alliance, a rag-tag bunch of fighters who have spent most of their time fighting each other after the retreat of the Soviet army, and whose short-lived reign in Kabul was well-known for its ferocity.

The Northern Alliance (now called the United Front), the Rome group (loyal to the exiled King), the Peshawar group (mainly Pashtu-speakers) and the Cyprus group (backed by Iran) met in Bonn from 27 November 2001 under the auspices of the United Nations to create a new regime in Afghanistan. Under the gun from the Europeans and the US, the meeting was told that if they did not come to an agreement they would forfeit financial support to rebuild the state. The stakes are high, since the total funds promised for a new regime come to between $8 and $10 billion, a figure that will be clarified in Tokyo in late January 2002. German Foreign Minister Joschka Fischer welcomed the parties on the first day with the inducement that without an agreement the parties can forget the more than $70 million pledged by the Germans toward the new regime (this violates the spirit of Article 52 of the 1969 Vienna Convention on the Law of Treaties, that a treaty does not hold if it is 'procured by the threat or use of force' – if we include economic force). With money such as this in the offing, it is important to stress that only a government acceptable to the donors will be allowed to be formed. Indeed, this is the reason that the meeting ended by being contentious from afar, even as the delegates at Bonn seemed optimistic. The new interim cabinet sidelined the Jamait-i-Islami boss Professor Burhanuddin Rabbani, a man close to Iran and Russia, two powers that are not trusted by the donor states.[31] An angry Rabbani told the press on 12 December that the cabinet is 'an insult to the Afghan nation'. From Mazar-e-Sharif, General Dostam (on 6 December) said, 'We are very sad. We announce a boycott of this government and will not go to

Kabul until there is a proper government in place'. Wahidullah Sabawoon of the Hizb-i-Islami asked that the Bonn accord be rewritten so that the Hizb have at least one ministerial berth. Haji Abdul Qadar, the Pashtun governor of Jalalabad, stormed out of the meeting because of 'inadequate Pashtun representation', but also because of this general dissatisfaction with the level of autonomy given to Afghanistan in the deliberations (that Dostam's militia murdered 600 Taliban prisoners of war on November 9 helped intensify the Pashtun sense of distrust in the Northern Alliance, just as the renewal of warlordism in Kandahar muted the Pashtun claim to being a distinct voice in the process).

The newly appointed head of the cabinet is the clan leader of the Popalzai, Hamid Karzai. Karzai's political teeth come from his biography within this important clan of the Pashtu speakers, but also from his role in the anti-Soviet jihad, even as he was mainly in the diplomatic and not military side of things. When the Taliban came to power, Karzai welcomed them and helped them with a financial donation (his family, meanwhile, sought refuge in the US and now run a successful chain of Afghan restaurants down its eastern coast; Karzai, during the Fourth Afghan War ran a hotel in Peshawar). Since then he turned against the Taliban's links to the ISI and the Afghan Arabs, and he became one of the pieces of the aborted Southern Alliance.[32] Backed by the UK, and given legitimacy by his social position, Karzai emerged as a compromise candidate from among the majority Pashtu speakers and the various minority groups (Tajiks, Uzbeks and Hazaras) who dominate the Northern Alliance. The young troika within the Northern Alliance (Foreign Minister Dr. Abdullah Abdullah, Defence Minister General Mohammed Fahim and Interior Minister Younis Qanooni) took the side of Karzai with the hope that a youthful cabinet may take Afghanistan out of the morass of the past. Of course, the Bonn meeting was hardly fresh blood, since the Northern Alliance is given legitimacy by the old warlords, the Rome group came with the King's blessings, the Peshawar group was headed by Hamid Gailani (son of a prominent head of the Sufis of Afghanistan) and the Cyprus group was led by Humayun Jareer, son-in-law of Gulbuddin Hikmatyar. Karzai himself is the son of Abdul Ahad Karzai, popular head of the Popalzai tribe. The crucial thing about Karzai (and this was also recognized by Rabbani in his attempt to sideline the Bonn meeting), however, is that while he may be an honest man, he is relatively powerless and will be seen as a puppet of international interests. For instance, although the US State Department reluctantly supported Karzai from November onwards (mainly to keep open the thesis that the 'moderate Taliban' may remain in the new government, a sop to Musharraf and the ISI), Karzai has maintained strong connections with the CIA ever since he met CIA director William Casey in the mid-1980s.[33]

The roots of the Northern Alliance, meanwhile, can be traced to the defection of General Abdul Rashid Dostam with his Uzbek militia from leftist President Najibullah's side in March 1992 – with this act the decimated People's Democratic Party of Afghanistan's days were numbered. The mujahideen entered Kabul and, in mid-April, they circumvented an immediate continuation of the war with a Peshawar alliance headed by Professor Rabbani. By August of 1992, the war began again, as Hikmatyar's Hezb-i-Islami took on the Professor's regime, and the ensuing instability resulted in the final demise of Najibullah's government in December. In March 1993, the factions conducted the Islamabad Accord so that Rabbani continued as President, while Hikmatyar became Prime Minister. But Hikmatyar was a poor ally, because he continued his terror, in alliance with the Hezb-i-Wahdat and in opposition to Rabbani (whose troops remained in the command of the late Ahmed Shah Masud, but who worked in cooperation with Dostam). In January 1994, Hikmatyar formed an alliance with Dostam, and so the musical chairs continued until Bonn. Hikmatyar, with Dostam, then with Masud, then Rabbani in the background – all the while the Taliban consolidated power, took Mazar-i-Sharif in 1997 and then finally Kabul. As the civil war unfolded the Northern

Alliance inflicted massive pain on the Afghan population. In January 1997, Dostam's forces ruthlessly bombed Kabul and Masud's forces continued to do so, even the day after 9/11 in retaliation for his assassination three days earlier.[34] After 9/11, this history was re-written by the powers mainly because the Northern Alliance now appeared as a reasonable alternative. That many of the Northern Alliance cultivated Iran was not to be a stumbling block, particularly after the slow, but steady US–Iran rapprochement during the second Clinton presidency. The Northern Alliance and the Taliban are certainly not identical, since the former, at the very least, do not oppose education for women, but the difference between them should not be exaggerated to forget the role played by the Northern Alliance in the devastation of contemporary Afghanistan. Karzai, during these years, played a double game, even asking Mullah Omar of the Taliban for a role as Afghanistan's envoy to the UN.

For Afghanistan, the US war aims are simultaneously as brutal and unfocused as in Iraq, although the interests at stake are quite clear – the restoration of 'stability' in the name of capital and in the interests of US imperialism (and we will get to the details of this oily business in the next chapter).

But the war aims are not only about Afghanistan, for they are also reflected in the economic aims of the aftermath of 9/11 and of the war. An early act of structural terrorism took place in the late 1950s as the mandarins of New York City began the procedures that led to the creation of the World Trade Center. Apart from the shenanigans to gain federal and municipal tax breaks, the Rockefeller family and the Downtown Lower Manhattan Association executed the eviction of the electrical district from New York, and thereby stealing almost thirty thousand people their jobs. A working-class New York was recomposed into the New York of FIRE – finance, insurance and real estate.[35] But this is ancient history as far as we are concerned ('you can't make an omelet without breaking some eggs', just as long as the eggs are working-class people and not the establishment). As Bill Clinton left office in mid-January 2001, news from the main economists in the US was that a recession was in the works (in the last week of November 2001, the US economy officially went into a recession). But the terror of 9/11 provided many large firms with the necessary excuse to slash jobs, even as many of these layoffs had been planned months in advance. The airlines led the way: 30,000 from Boeing, 20,000 each from American Airlines and United, and a host of other cuts (including five thousand white-collar jobs at Ford, and almost nine thousand employees at Cisco Systems). As the tragedy of 9/11 greets a lakh of workers with the pink-slips of unemployment, this has put a damper on consumer confidence; and since consumer spending accounts for two-thirds of all economic activity in the US, the lay-offs furthered the US entry into a recession; and since the US is the buyer of the last resort of planetary capitalism, this set the financial markets around the world on edge. A total disaster was circumvented by oil prices, now the lowest in two years and kept low by Saudi and Russian assistance (both refuse to curtail production and raise the general price). The economic terror is a conjunctural aftermath of the terror of 9/11, but it also has its own terrorist dynamic, the desire for profit above human need. The analysis of *Das Kapital* is proved right as the woes of DOS Capital become general.

Even as their colleagues lay dead under the rubble of the WTC, the stockbrokers went at it soon afterwards to salvage profits from a shaky market. The significant drop in the Dow Jones was soon to be bolstered by consumer confidence in the war industries, in security firms (including in those that produce flak jackets) and in the construction sector. There is money to be made off tragedy. Indeed, to make money has always been a value in the US, and now, after 9/11, US residents inhabit a state of 'market patriotism', a term well-coined by the former US Secretary of Labour Robert Reich. 'We demonstrate our resolve to the rest of the world by investing and consuming at least as much as we did before, preferably more', Reich wrote shortly after 9/11.[36] 'The terrorists tried to strike at the heart of American capitalism', he wryly continued. 'We show that

American capitalism is alive and well by giving it as much of our credit card as possible.' As consumer debt spirals out of control (consumer debt as a percentage of disposable income is now 97 per cent, whereas it was 68 per cent in 1980), and becomes the domestic version of Third World debt (now approximately $3 trillion), the President asks that people sacrifice any hope of fiscal responsibility toward the greater good of the military-industrial-fiscal complex.

Anticipation of the economic downturn drew President Bush to a forthright call for 'market patriotism'. On 20 September, he told the country that 'I ask you to live your lives and hug your children', and he asked for 'continued participation and confidence in the American economy'. Keep up with the Dow Joneses, said the President, and heal with an upswing in the flag-draped market. But, unlike other moments in US history during wartimes, the sacrifice being called for is consumerism and a complete capitulation to the neoliberal strategy of the Right: US Trade Representative Robert Zoellick argued that this is the perfect time for the US Congress to relinquish authority to the president to conduct trade deals. 'Economic strength at home and abroad is the foundation of America's hard and soft power', he wrote. 'Earlier enemies learned that America is the arsenal of democracy. Today's enemies will learn that America is the economic engine for freedom, opportunity and development. To that end, US leadership in promoting the international economic and trading system is vital. Trade is about more than economic efficiency. It promotes the values at the heart of this protracted struggle'.[37] The specific treaties in question are the expansion of NAFTA into the Free Trade Area of the Americas, a compact that has provoked enormous protests from the Southern Cone to Quebec, and the incorporation of African nations into the Africa Growth and Opportunity Act, a treaty greatly resented by many Africans. Terrorism plays directly into the hands of US imperialism, as it allows it to dry its tears with dollar bills and force the world to sign off on our differences as consolation for the attacks of nineteen men.

A restructured economic compact between the US state and its citizens is not the only domestic war aim, for the other one is a transformed relationship with immigrants and with civil liberties. A few hours after the suicide attack on the WTC and the Pentagon, a combination of official and unofficial acts against those with brown skin took place across the United States.

Within minutes after the WTC attacks, angry white men yelled obscenities and chased Amrik Singh Chawla of Brooklyn, New York, down the street, and his only escape was to hide his turban in his briefcase. In the small state of Rhode Island, officials stopped a train, handcuffed a Sikh man and removed him from the train. He was detained primarily because of his turban and skin color, perhaps all he shares with Osama bin Laden. Indeed, this Sikh man's turmoil was to be visited on Sikhs across the United States. Within a few days, Sikh community organizations and civil rights groups reported over fifty attacks against Sikhs. A white man assaulted an elderly Sikh man who was then taken to the hospital, just as unknown assailants firebombed a Sikh gurudwara near Cleveland, Ohio. The day after the WTC attack, train officials and the police removed Meera Kumar and a group of South Asians and Arabs from a Boston-New York train. Two days later, at a meeting organized by the South Asian Journalists Association in New York to discuss the hate crimes, a man who was taking his baby on a walk assaulted one of the Sikh participants. 'You Islamic mosquitoes should be killed', he yelled, a phrase captured by TV Asia and run on its show through the day. 'Americans saw *Lawrence of Arabia* and think all Muslims wear turbans', said Kevin Fitzpatrick, an organizer with the New York Taxi Workers Alliance. Manga Singh, a taxi driver, reported to NYTWA that a passenger started to beat him with an umbrella while yelling, 'I hate you, I hate you and your turban'. Mr. Singh's father, Surinder Singh, is also a taxi driver and he reported that a rider said to him, 'You did that, you attacked the World Trade Center'. One Sikh man, Balbir Singh Sodhi, a worker at a all-night store, was shot to death in Mesa, Arizona, by a man who told the police, 'I stand for America all the way'.

Hours after Mr. Sodhi was found dead, an unknown assailant shot Waqar Hassan of Dallas, Texas. Mr. Hassan was at work as a store clerk at Mom's Grocery when he was shot. Mosques joined gurudwaras in the saturnalia of random violence, just as South and West Asians of all faiths began to join Sikhs as targets of retaliation for the WTC. The bulk of the attacks took place not against all those who are of West and South Asian descent, but against the working-class and small merchant sector amongst them. Those who worked the lonely, long-hour jobs at kiosks or in taxis faced the wrath of their customers, while the ethnic neighbourhoods (generally peopled by the working class) became a visible target for retaliation. The professionals whose homes are lost in the thicket of white suburbs faced suspicious looks and suffered the indignity of racism, but no significant physical violence. Mr. Ashraf Khan, for instance, is a cell-phone magnate. He was removed from a first-class seat on a Delta Airlines aircraft because the pilot felt that he endangered the plane. The fear set in amongst all classes, even as the working-class bore the brunt of the retaliatory violence. The volume of the attacks was not enormous, and yet a general sense of fear pervaded South and West Asians in the US. Many refused to leave their homes, to go to work or to school, and many foreign students got on the first plane back to their homelands.

Things got so bad, so fast, that President Bush had to make an appearance at a Washington DC mosque on September 17 to mollify South Asians and Arabs, as well as to say 'those who feel they can intimidate our fellow Americans by taking out their anger, they don't represent the best of America'. Indeed, the US media began to run stories about how ordinary Muslims did not feel kin with the WTC attacks, indeed that most Muslims condemned them and that Islam is a faith of peace. Speaking from both sides of the same mouth, the same media wrote in rabid tones about Islam in general, a ploy to dehumanize the 'enemy' before the October 7 bombardment.

President Bush's statement, however, was made hollow the next day by Attorney General Ashcroft's announcement. He informed the country that whereas previously the Immigration and Naturalization Service (INS) could only hold an 'alien that had been taken into custody because of a violation' for twenty-four hours, the new regulation would allow the INS to hold the 'alien' for 'forty-eight hours, or to an additional reasonable time'. In one swoop, the Justice Department revoked the right of habeas corpus for non-citizens of the US, and it allowed officers of the Law to turn any 'violation' (not a guilty verdict) into an excuse for indefinite detention. Ashcroft's rules, which will be challenged in federal court because they are against the US constitution, have made official the tenor of the unofficial attacks on West and South Asians. And then, in November, the US government passed the USA Patriot Act that allowed authorities to take undue liberties with immigrants, who may be held in indefinite detention or deported on the Justice Department's authority (that is, without judicial oversight). The FBI may now conduct routine secret searches, and it allows them, without judicial review, to monitor and arrest individuals who have not yet committed a crime, but who the government believes *may* do so. There is no presupposition of innocence until proven guilty in this new directive. In late November, Bush announced an executive order to try suspected terrorists who are not citizens in military tribunals (that is, without the niceties of bourgeois legality). The domestic war aim is to use the WTC attacks as pretext for the increased repression of certain population groups, whether those of colour or else those who dissent from the right-wing thrust in the US.

The war took place in passive voice, but the suffering produced by it is active, very active.

4

Tolerance of Arabia

> Arab oil has corrupted the Arab condition not only in the oil lands, but in the Arab world as a whole.
>
> Abdelrahman Munif[1]

I. AMNESIA AND INNOCENT AMERICA

We live in times of great amnesia. The Taliban forgets that it alone did not make the Soviet Army retreat, the leftist government collapse, and then the warlords leave Kabul for exile. Amnesia about its allies, the CIA, the Saudis and the ISI makes it overestimate its own rather impoverished capacity to stand up to the immense might of the US–UK military. The technological superiority of the US forces and its smooth capacity to get the natives to do the ground war themselves (the Northern Alliance here, the Iraqi National Congress and the southern Shi'a in Iraq) cannot be matched by scattershot armaments and the depleted ordinance of the Taliban army. The rather pathetic maps on the military command centres of the Taliban in Kabul and its reliance on the internet for data on bombs and on US movements shows that the Taliban was severely outclassed on the battlefield by the technology and the diplomacy of the US.[2]

But the US too suffers from acute amnesia.[3] Washington is eager to deny its role both in the facilitation of the Taliban to power and of the entry of such people as Osama bin Laden to the centre of world politics. I have a fantasy about being given access to the archives of the CIA at Langley, Virginia. Somewhere in the vault I'd find the first edition (perhaps from the late 1940s) of a manual that has been copied many times, since the thoroughly effective CIA would have used it almost every few years. Like other manuals it would probably be bound in a bold colour with large black letters that say something like, 'Manual for Counter-Insurgency: How to Manufacture an Enemy Who Once Was an Asset'. In the files that go with the manual, we'd find one on President Manuel Noriega, a valuable CIA asset inside the Panamanian military right up to the invasion of the country in December 1989 when the marines arrested the sovereign, but corrupt leader and incarcerated him in the US. In 1983 Noreiga met with Vice President G.H. Bush to discuss allegations of drug dealing and money-laundering, but for the next six years the US did little to disrupt the lucrative business of its ally. When populist forces arose in Panama to contest the US hold on the crucial canal and the US bases, Washington and then President Bush discarded their ally, charged him with crimes that it tacitly supported and sent in the marines. The invasion of Panama was a preview of the Gulf War.

But imperialism is supple, seeking new tactics in new moments, finding ways to intervene to undermine the political dynamic of genuine democracy in the name of 'democracy' and 'human rights'. Few interventions are identical to others, since these are worked out carefully, often with the connivance of local elites, eager to hold onto power at all costs, at any cost. Since the end of the Second World War, when the US became the buyer of last resort and the principle pole for US–European imperialism, it has feared three foes – the Soviet Union, radical nationalisms of all sorts, and national communist parties in the Third World.[4] The US joined hands with any outrageous villain, whether Mobuto in the Congo or Marcos in the Philippines as long as this alliance crushed any aspiration for the nationalization of a country's wealth and produce, checked the growth of Soviet power, and destroyed the workers and peasants movements, themselves frequently led by national communist parties. There is a game plan at work, but it works differently in different settings; the context for this book is Afghanistan, and the fulcrum of its destiny lies in the distant peninsula of Saudi Arabia. Yes, Afghanistan is related to Arabia since the seventh century, when the people of Ghor sent a holy man by the name of Kais to greet the prophet Muhammad only nine years after he had announced his mission; Kais returned with Islam, the first gift from Arabia. The link that this book traces does not immediately start with Kais, for it is more inclined to spend time on Afghanistan's place as the hub of the anti-Soviet mission of the US, the Saudis and their junior partner, the Pakistanis (from 1979 to 1989), as an outpost of dissent against the rule of the Saudi royal family (since 1991, at least), and as the terrain for a potentially lucrative oil and natural gas pipeline from Central Asia.

None of this is to indulge the conspiracy theories that the Saudis or the CIA or Mossad orchestrated 9/11. This is quite far-fetched. Indeed, the Saudis grand mufti, Sheikh Abd al-Aziz bin Abdallah al-Shaykh, prohibited suicide attacks in the name of Islam as recently as 21 April 2001.[5] The point is that the tolerance of Arabia encouraged by the US and facilitated by Pakistani action (whether at Black September in 1970 or else in the harbouring of the *mehmeen* mujahideen) produced the social conditions that spawned the terror of 9/11. If those social conditions are not addressed and redressed, it is likely that there will be more, tragic 9/11s in the future.

II. THE ASSASSINATION OF NASSERISM

In 1965, the ex-President of Ghana, Kwame Nkrumah wrote a book that was fated to be a classic, but has since been forgotten, *Neocolonialism: The Last Stage of Imperialism*. Nkrumah recognized that the period of colonial racism was over, the time when European rulers captured lands and peoples of Asia, Africa and Latin America to make them work for the profit of Northwestern Europe and the United States. With the freedom of the erstwhile colonies, the corporations and corporate states had to find a new means to dominate the world. Formerly colonized people had the right to rule over themselves politically, but economic sovereignty over them was still to be dictated by Europe. 'The essence of neocolonialism is that the State which is subject to it is, in theory, independent and has all the outward trappings of international sovereignty. In reality its economic system and thus its political policy is directed from outside.'[6] If Europe and the US held that bourgeois democracy was the hallmark of modernity, they simultaneously held that those whom they deemed to be (either racially or culturally) inferior should have other ways to rule themselves. This form of multi-racist treatment enabled the US to justify their alliances with ruthless dictators *in the name of cultural relativism*, just as long as these dictators submitted the destiny of their own states to that of the corporatized state of the US. European and US support for the ruthless emirates in the Gulf, of which Saudi Arabia is the leader, must be seen as part of the multi-racist foreign policy of US–Europe in neocolonial times. Arabs, we are told, are unable to create a democracy because of their cultural heritage of tribalism, so that the US–Europe can only encourage the emirs, and slowly shepherd them to something constitutional. For now, however, the US–Europe will offer military and economic aid to prop up unscrupulous kings (for the Arabs and the Persians) and ruthless dictators (for the Africans). US support of the Shah of Iran, of the Emirs of the Gulf States and of Jordan, of Mobuto in the Congo and of other such figures illustrates the racist practice of neocolonialism.

Furthermore, on the track of race again, the best way for the US–UK to indict the Arabs (and Islam) in general is not to have establishment-inducted scholars talk about imperialism's possessive investment in tribalism but to talk about a 'clash of civilizations' (Samuel Huntington) or else about 'the revolt of Islam' (Bernard Lewis). Islam, like any other faith practice, has its problems, but in our contemporary world it has come to represent the antithesis of modernity. The stereotypes about Islam feed our belief that there are those who live in feudal times, and the US–UK governments must be given the freedom to deal with them as if it ruled as medieval lords. There is no conflict between Jihad and McWorld, because Jihad is as modern as our current globalization – emblazoned on the banners of the Islamicists are not only slogans of the past, but (in invisible ink) the words Oil, Natural Gas and Frustrated Dreams of Freedom. And an end to the petro-dynasties that rule over a tenth of the Arabs and refuse to share the spoils of oil.

Ibn Saud, the founder of Saudi Arabia, was a brigand before he was encouraged by the English to take leadership against the Ottoman Empire. Long before he became King (1932), the English monarch knighted him (1915) and just after his accession to the newly fabricated emirate of Arabia, the monarch of England bestowed upon him the Order of the Bath (1935). English advisors sat beside him, people such as Henry St. John Philby (father of the Soviet spy, Kim Philby) and Sir John Baggot Glubb (known as Glubb Pasha). In the 1920s, the English helped arm Ibn Saud as his Ikhwan ('brothers') took inspiration from the fanatical Wahhabism (a branch of Sunni Islam developed in the eighteenth century by the Ibn Saud family's patron saint Sheikh Muhammad ibn Abdul Wahhab) and executed not less than four hundred thousand people to give Ibn Saud dominance over the Arabian Peninsula. Glubb Pasha said of this that 'Ibn Saud used the massacre to subdue his enemies', this in a land of only four million.[7] North of Arabia, the British installed Faisal (son of Sharif Husain of Hijaz) to rule over Iraq, a Sunni leader over a predominantly Shi'a land. In 1932, as Iraq became an independent state, the Anglo-Iraq treaty took effect by which the British held onto the airfields of Habbaniyya and Shu'ayba so that they might better control their puppet king.[8]

Oil, the liquid gold, was only discovered in large quantities once Ibn Saud named the country after himself and took sole title to it. Afraid of a rebellion from below and eager for funds to lavish pleasure on his seven thousand-member royal family, Ibn Saud signed treaties with US–British oil firms and began a relationship that continues to this day – the Saudis act as rentiers of a reservoir that holds a quarter of the world's oil; they control production so that the price of oil does not rise to Britain–US's disadvantage; they use any means to thwart a challenge to their domination, this in order to protect the passage of oil. The sovereignty of the masses is curtailed by the mendacious arrangement made by imperialism and its franchise, here the Ibn Saud family.

The challenge to the oil kings came from Nasserism and communism. Communism had an early start in the oil lands, with the main parties being formed in Palestine (1919), Iran (1920), Egypt (1922), and Iraq (1932). The Iranians came to communism from two sources, the migrant workers in the Baku oil fields who met Bolsheviks there and translated the *Communist Manifesto*'s line, 'workers of the world, unite' into Farsi, *kargaran-e-jahan mottahad shaweed*, and people such as Ahmed Sultanzadeh, an important presence at the Congress of the Toilers of the East at Baku in 1920. The Palestinian, Egyptian and Iraqi parties were well served by the intellectual Jewish community, by the presence of rational military officers, and by workers in sectors of the economy that came under pressure from imperialism.[9] The tenacity and bravery of the communists in the face of imperialist aggression won them many adherents. In early 1948, for example, when the Iraqis and the British almost signed the Portsmouth treaty which made the relationship between the powers more equal, but still allowed the British access to airfields, the Iraqi Communist Party emerged not only as the main force against the treaty, but as the main opposition to the regime. When the state cracked down on the ICP, the dead bodies of the ICP members that hung around the capital 'surrounded [Iraqi communism] with the halo of martyrdom'.[10] The ICP was not only the oldest party in Iraq, but by the 1940s its doctrines had 'spread so widely in the big towns', said chief of police Bahjat 'Atiyyah, that 'nearly fifty per cent of the youthful elements of all classes had been carried away by them'.[11] And when Dr. Muhammed Mossadegh (*Time* magazine's man of the year in 1951) won the elections in Iran to become Prime Minister in 1951, he welcomed the Iranian Communist Party to his side mainly to give him ballast as he nationalized the oil fields and enraged the British and their elves. Even as the CIA exaggerated Mossadegh's own relationship with the Iranian Communist Party, a secret history of the CIA's role in Iran written by Dr. Donald Wilber in 1954 reported that Allen Dulles (director of the CIA) authorized $1 million to overthrow Mossadegh and 'bring to power a government which would reach an equitable oil settlement, enabling Iran to become economically sound and financially solvent, and which would vigorously prosecute the dangerously strong Communist Party'.[12] Eventually only a tenth of the $ 1 million was actually spent – a very cheap coup. It should also be pointed out that the Shah's army acted against the Communists prior to the coup, mainly because of the royalists fears at the strength of the Iranian Communist Party by 1953.

Mossadegh's victory in 1951 and the subsequent nationalization of the oil fields (as well as his astute use of the new media, particularly the radio, to reach the masses) impressed a generation of leaders in neighbouring Arab lands, notably in Egypt. There, on 23 July 1952, a group of twelve military officers staged a *coup d'état* against the monarchy, called themselves the Free Officers, and took power under the leadership of Gamel Abdul Nasser. The Free Officers, like the FLN in Algeria, came to power without a coherent political programme, even as they drew from the popular notion of pan-Arabism (*al-qawmiyya al-'arabiyyai*). Pan-Arabism developed from such important intellectuals as the Syrian Satia al-Husri (1880–1968), who produced a nationalist ethos through a close reading of Arab history and of German Romanticism. The combination of the two allowed al-Husri to argue that the Arab nation was not to be produced, but that it was organic and needed simply to be brought to life. An utter secularist, al-Husri believed that the language of Arabic and an Arab culture predated Islam, and it is this that should be the basis for the Arab nation (whatever political shape this nation might take).[13] Nasser, two decades afterwards, was to be the heroic individual destined to awaken the nation.

Indeed, Nasser created a flurry in the Arab world, and in the Third World in general. On 14 August 1958, Prime Minister Nehru assessed the rise of Arab nationalism before the Lok Sabha. 'In a very powerful, resurgent way', he told the house, 'Egypt took the lead in this matter and, under the wise leadership of President Nasser, has played a very important part. Nasser, in fact, became the most prominent symbol of Arab nationalism. This fact, which was patent, was neither liked nor appreciated by many powers, and an attempt was made to split the Arab countries, in fact, Arab nationalism'. Always alert to the contradictions of international relations, Nehru pointed out that *before* Nasser nationalized the Suez canal (1956) the US and the United Kingdom created the Baghdad Pact (1954), nominally to check the USSR, but really to undermine Arab nationalism. 'In the countries associated with the Baghdad Pact', Nehru continued, 'there was a hiatus between the Governments and the people, the people looking more and more towards Arab nationalism and the Governments looking in another direction and rather ranged against this spirit of Arab nationalism. How big the hiatus was can be seen from the *coup d'état* in Baghdad which surprised everyone.' On 14 July 1958, two hundred Free Officers (as they fashioned themselves) overthrew the monarchy and Brigadier Abd al-Karim Qasim, a Nasserite, became Prime Minister – Arab nationalism of a Nasserite stamp was still on the rise.

Nasserism found a close ally in most Arab lands among the vibrant communist parties, mainly because most Nasserite governments came to power as the military overthrew a corrupt monarchy, and these military officers needed civilian organizations to execute their programmes in society. The organization of the communist parties became essential in the early years of progressive Nasserism, whether in Egypt, Iraq, Syria or even later in Sudan. But while Nasserism took advantage of the communist organization, the programme of Nasserism was far too ambiguous to allow full communist participation. In Egypt, for example, the Free Officers' coup was led by people of vastly different political outlooks, from those who remained close to the Muslim Brotherhood (the Ikhwan) to those who found fellowship in the Egyptian Communist Party (known as the Hadeto in those years, an Arabic acronym for the Democratic Movement for National Liberation).[14] The B'aath Party of Syria and then Iraq fought the communists for ideological control of the nascent Pan-Arabism. The 24 July 1943 programme of the Ba'ath movement (the first to be released), and written by the Syrian founder of the party, Michel 'Aflaq, frankly stated, 'We represent the Arab spirit against materialist communism'. Furthermore, he wrote, 'communism is Western, and alien to everything Arab'.[15] Ten days after the Free Officers' coup in Baghdad, 'Aflaq arrived there to try and draw Qasim toward the Ba'ath and against the Iraqi Communist Party. After the coup, the Iraqi Communist Party cadres numbered 25,000 and the members in mass organizations totalled half a million. The Ba'ath of Iraq at that time was only three hundred in 1956, and then about three thousand after the coup. All the unions, the Popular Resistance Front (a civilian militia) and most youth organizations pledged their fealty to the Iraqi Communist Party, and when it was under threat, an enormous demonstration of at least half a million people took place on 1 May 1959 to demand communist representation in the government. The Qasim government, under pressure from the Ba'ath began to repress the Communist party (and the Kurds in the north, who formed a communist bastion) only to fall himself to a Ba'athist coup on 8 February 1963.

The rise of both Nasserism and communism terrified the oil royals and the states of imperialism. In January 1957, Ibn Saud, son of the founder of Saudi Arabia, travelled to Washington, DC, to meet with US President Eisenhower and they produced a declaration known as the Eisenhower Doctrine (to protect Saudi Arabia as if it were part of the USA). Even as Eisenhower found Ibn Saud personally unfit for leadership, he accepted that this substandard leader was the stuff that allowed the oil to travel untrammeled by nationalists like Nasser. The meeting took place after Nasser nationalized the Suez Canal in 1956, thereby putting all ship traffic between Asia and Europe at the mercy of the Egyptian state; in response the British and French invaded the Suez. That year Nasser traveled to Riyadh (Saudi Arabia), where the people received him as a hero. 'Arab Oil For the Arab People', said Nasser, and he not only scared the US government (who invaded Lebanon in 1958), but also local potentates (such as the heads of Iraq and Lebanon) who, in the words of the Fouad Ajami 'reign, but do not rule'. The animus against Nasser was so great that in March 1958 the Saudi royal family, it is said, attempted to assassinate him by having his plane shot down as it approached a landing at Damascus.

The CIA went into action, alongside Saudi intelligence and money. In 1957, the CIA helped the Jordanian King Hussein overthrow the popularly elected Nasserite cabinet; Saudi troops went to Jordan to help maintain Hussein's kingdom just as the US Sixth Fleet entered the eastern Mediterranean to send a signal to Nasserism. The United States provided $10 million as the first installment to boost the economy and military of Jordan, the latter mainly staffed by a ruthless Bedouin army (who became useful in September 1970 alongside a Pakistani detachment commanded by General Zia-ul Haq that murdered a vast section of the Palestinian Liberation Organization who then took refuge in Lebanon). In January 1958, Egypt, Syria and Yemen joined to form the United Arab Republic, a formation that put immense political pressure on the governments of the Arab lands since now the people began to demand that their states join in this pan-Arab union. The Jordanian and Iraqi monarchies, in haste, created the Hashemite Union to counter the UAR, but this was short-lived due to the Qasim coup some months later. Under pressure in Lebanon, the right wing murdered a left-wing newspaper reporter on 8 May 1958, an act that called out the people in a general strike the next day. Under pressure President Chamille Chamoun ran to the United Nations and on 15 July, the US Sixth Fleet sent marines to Beirut and put in place Operation Bluebat (planned long before the Suez crisis of 1956, but the representatives of the US Army, Navy and Air force of Mediterranean met in London during September 1957 to refine the plans, including a marine assault on Lebanon rather than an airdrop into Jordan, among other things).

The military intervention sent an overt message that the US interests must not be trampled, but meanwhile the CIA conducted covert activities to bolster the opposition to Nasserism. The CIA was not alone in this, being partnered at each step by Saudi intelligence, the famous al-Istakhbara al-'Ama. Many of the tactical moves of the CIA had been worked out during the 1953 coup against Mossadegh in Iran. In early August, the CIA's Iranian operatives pretended to be members of the Communist Party as they threatened senior Muslim leaders with 'savage punishment if they opposed Mossadegh', so as to rally the Muslim clerics against the communists; CIA operatives bombed at least at least one house of a well-regarded Muslim cleric, again posing as communists. Kermit Roosevelt, Teddy Roosevelt's grandson, was dispatched to oversee the coup and he spent as little as $100,000 to marshal a demonstration against the regime that marched to Mossadegh's office and attacked him.[16] In Egypt, the Muslim Brotherhood (ancestor of Osama bin Laden's current collaborator, the Islamic Jihad) received CIA funds to undermine Nasser; in eastern Saudi Arabia, journalist Saïd Aburish claims, CIA agent James Russell Barracks confirmed the existence of 'an extensive programme' to fund small religious cells (these are the direct ancestors of bin Laden's Advice and Reformation Committee or Hayat Annaseyha Wa'ahisla)[17]; finally, in Iraq, the Secretary General of the Ba'ath Party noted that 'we came to power on an American train' in 1963, both through direct funds (alongside Kuwaiti money) and through the use of CIA-run radio stations in Kuwait that broadcasted anti-communist messages from an Islamic fundamentalist standpoint into a secular and socialist Iraq (among these anti-communist Ba'ath leaders stood Saddam Hussein).

In 1965, the Saudi monarch Faisal convened an International Islamic Conference in Mecca where the Saudis unveiled their World Muslim League (Rabita al-Alam al-Islami). The Muslim Brotherhood told the gathering, 'Those who distort Islam's call under the guise of nationalism are the most bitter enemies of the Arabs, whose glories are entwined with the glories of Islam'. The Brotherhood invoked the idea of *shu'ubi* (anti-Arab) to cast aspersions specifically at Nasserism (or pan-Arabism) and communism. There are direct echoes here of the anti-communist arguments of the Ba'athist 'Alfaq and of the intellectual guide to the Sudanese National Islamic Front, Dr. Hasan al-Turabi ('Today if you want to assert indigenous values, originality and independence against the West, then Islam is the only doctrine'[18]). The combination of anti-communism and pro-Islam developed by the Saudis and their Islamicist allies appealed greatly to the United States government, so much that the head of the Brotherhood, Sayed Kuttub wryly called Islamism 'American made Islam'. In 1970, Faisal's activities culminated in the Organization of Islamic Conference with its current headquarters in Jeddah, and a strong alternative to any pan-Arabist tendencies. The road was open to the most virulent forms of Sunni Islam to take precedence over all that is beautiful in both heterodox Islam and in the democratic urges of the Arab people. The Saudis used a right-wing form of Sunni populism to quell the resentment among a population that suffers the indignity of poverty. Even as oil bathed the Ibn Saud family with wealth, the people of the peninsula suffered from neglect: there was neither the development of the physical plant of the country, nor of the intellectual capacity of the people (the literacy rate is about 55 per cent). When King Faisal was asked about women's education, which is almost non-existent for the majority, he said that women would get equal rights and opportunities 'when we grant them to men'.[19] The Ibn Saud clan posed as chiefs of Islam at home, as they became famously mischief men abroad (the activities of the Saudi family, whether in the casinos or in the up-scale brothels is the stuff of legend): the Saudi royals 'should have more fear of God', said one of the Islamists. 'On the one hand they pray but in the other they pick up the bottle'.[20]

If much of the decimation of pan-Arabism came from the production of an Islamism wedded to anti-American themes, in Iraq the demise of the left was from the deformations within pan-Arabism itself. 'Alfaq's anti-communism enabled the transformation of the Iraqi Ba'ath agenda during the decade of the 1960s (from the coup of 1963 to the coup of 1968). After the second coup, when Saddam Hussein took power, he intervened in the split within the communist movement – the pro-Soviet party joined the regime, as the Ba'ath's militia (the *Jihaz Haneen*) took out the militant Iraqi Communist Party (Central Leadership). Incidentally, Saddam Hussein turned on the pro-Soviet party in 1978–79 after its usefulness had come to an end. Saddam Hussein's first chief of Internal Security, Nadhim Kzar, enthusiastically arrested, tortured and killed cadre from the ICP and from among the left-wing Kurdish liberation movements. For decades the communist movement grew amongst the Kurds, both in Turkey and in northern Iraq.[21] But by the early 1970s, the CIA entered the battlefield to cut down the left and bolster the right. Between 1972 and 1975 the CIA paid $16 million to the eccentric and untrustworthy Mullah Mustafa Barzani as a 'moral guarantee' of US support for his activities. In 1959, Barzani had expelled the communists from his mainly Iraqi party and he had sent Iranian Kurds to their death in the camps of the Shah. The spillover from the growth of Islamism bothered the Ba'ath, who remain quite secular, and in 1979 Saddam Hussein made an alliance with the Shah of Iran to quell the Islamists (in February 1963 the Shah had also helped the Ba'ath, mainly by turning over Iraqi democrats who fled the Ba'athist onslaught).

Barzani was an asset that the US cultivated, and is now a close ally of Saddam Hussein. In 1975, Marxist-Leninists within the Kurdish resistance formed the Patriotic Union of Kurdistan (PUK), which pushed many Kurds to the left, including those in the Iraqi Kurdish Front formed in 1988. Saddam Hussein was given the green light by Washington to take out the PUK, and he conducted chemical bombing on them in 1983 (at Arbil) and most spectacularly in 1988 (at Halabja, where five thousand died, and many thousand continue to suffer). This relationship entranced the US and the CIA, who saw Saddam Hussein as a factor of stability against both the Iranian revolution of 1979 and against Soviet influence in the region.

The growth of the Islamist elements certainly contributed to the demise of Nasserism, but the pan-Arabist dream also died from internal maladies.[22] Marie Christie Aulas showed us that the Nasserite project in Egypt, for example, was bereft of a programme. The regime's main intellectual was Mohammed Heikal, the editor of *Al-Ahram*, a man who was enamoured of W.W. Rostow's 'stages of economic growth', and who developed the theory of a 'non-capitalist road to development' that was essentially state capitalism.[23] Land reforms by the Nasser regime led to the transfer of land from the aristocratic landowners to rich peasants whose development was funded by the regime, just as the bulk of the peasantry remained landless. Not only did Nasserism fail the peasantry, it also did not aid in the creation of industry and an industrial work force. While less than twenty per cent of the increase in the workforce came from the manufacturing sector, the number of bureaucrats increased by over sixty per cent in the 1960s (their incomes rose by over two hundred per cent).[24] Pan-Arabism ruled from above, with a concentration on the creation of a strong state that regulated the lives of the people, rather than by awakening the aspirations of the people into democratic socialist organizations that would command the economic life of the country. Nasserism, then, not only lacked a programme to deal with the basic needs of the population, but it also lacked the will to devolve power to the people, to break the Pharonic structures bequeathed to it from the monarchy and from the military.

When Israel defeated the Arab armies in 1967, this put the nail in the coffin of Nasserism.

III. MCJIHAD VS. THE WORLD

Benjamin Barber's *Jihad Versus McWorld* intimates that the jihads are the antithesis of globalization, that the soulless corporation meets its antinomy in the fanatical fundamentalist.[25] Barber retools the modern–traditional dichotomy of modernization theory, so that while tradition used to be seen as a holdover into the modern period, Barber allows for the modernity of Jihad. Nevertheless, he suggests that globalization is set against 'Lebanonization', that the forces of transnational capital meet their bulwark in a defensive and cruel cultural nationalism. On the contrary, sectarian or cruel nationalism in the formerly colonized world is not only an adequate form of globalization, especially with the collapse of the socialist bloc, but that it seems to be the form that globalization takes in its current period. The BJP in India, Fox in Mexico, among others, show us that as the import-substitution type regimes lost their legitimacy as nationalist forces, then the cultural nationalist could reinvent themselves as patriotic forces even as they facilitated the entry of transnational capital and IMFundamentalism. Jihad is the Trojan Horse of globalization, which is why it might be better to collapse the dialectic couple Jihad and McWorld into the category of McJihad.

Egypt, like India, offers a test case for McJihad. Anwar al-Sadat took power of the Egyptian state at the death of Nasser in 1970. Sadat was a seasoned hand at the Janus-faced line of McJihad. From the late 1930s, the Egyptian army deputed Sadat to be its liaison with the right-wing Muslim Brotherhood (Jama'at al-Ikhwan al-Muslimoun, founded in 1928). The Ikhwan's leader Hasan al-Bana forged strong ties with the royal family through Sadat, and Sadat facilitated the Ikhwan's access to political resources such as cheap printers for propaganda materials, cheap land for mosques, and access to army camps to train the uniformed activists of the Ikhwan (*jawalla*) who formed its military battalions (*kata'ib*). The royal family used the Ikhwan to check the growth of the nationalist Wafd party, but in the long run the Ikhwan would become a far more important force than the Wafd.[26] Sadat kept up these links even as he became a central part of the Nasserite apparatus, and when he took power in 1970 he unleashed the Ikhwan into civil society to stifle any criticism of his actions.[27] The Ikhwan operated openly, took charge of the college campuses, began to dominate the mosques.[28] Sadat, meanwhile, fashioned himself as the Believer-President (*al-rais al-mou'min*) and ensured that the 1971 constitution declared that *Shari'a* is the 'principal source of legislation'.[29]

The other face of Sadat, meanwhile, unleashed IMFundamentalism on Egypt. Sadat's policy of *infatah* ('open door') liberalized the import-substitution type economic arrangements and welcomed transnational capital into the country. In 1974, *after the Egyptian victory over Israel in the Arab–Israeli war of 1973*, Sadat welcomed the creation of free trade zones along the Suez Canal (an affront to its 1956 nationalization) and he pushed through an investment law that opened the commanding areas of the economy (finance, industry, metallurgy and insurance) to foreign investment. This was the 'blood transfusion' that Sadat said Egypt needed.[30] The Egyptian economy went into a tailspin, mainly because the import bill now included mainly luxury goods (it increased from just under $4 billion in 1973 to almost $6 billion in 1976) and because an end to the subsidy of basic goods and a devaluation of the Egyptian pound created rampant inflation for the working class. In the decades after *infatah*, the educated youth found themselves in the category of the unemployed, as almost a quarter of Cairo's unemployed held university degrees.[31] The only way to balance the books was to take IMF assistance and to transform Egypt's relationship with the US – the Camp David accords of 1978 and Egypt's new role as the defender of the oil monarchies earned it the eternal gratitude from Washington which continues to maintain the Sadatian regime (now in Mubarak's hands) with billions of dollars in direct aid.

Across the Red Sea, the Saudi regime is another example of McJihad. When oil was discovered in the peninsula during the 1930s, the Arab American Oil Company (ARAMCO) dominated the oil reserves; US-based transnational energy firms played the main role in the consortium, and they reaped enormous revenues for decades. The Saudi regime remains beholden to the oil companies and to the US military, both of whom ensure the stability of the region for the traffic in oil. Like the Venezuelans[32] and the other oil lands, the Saudis reaped the windfall, but did little to develop the region for the betterment of their fellows. Profligate expenditure on personal consumption by the bloated royal family and for an increasingly showpiece military led to a collapse of the Saudi economy, with reserves falling from $121 billion (1984) to just under $51 billion (1993), and with a continued decline since then.[33] To maintain its legitimacy in the Arab world and among its increasingly disgruntled population, the Saudis pushed the notion of Islamic unity in opposition to pan-Arabism, it also funded right-wing Islamic groups across the Arabic speaking world (from the Algerian Islamic Front to undercut the FLN to Hamas to put pressure on the PLO), and in addition, the Saudi regime developed a religious police (*Mutawwa'in*) that resembled the Taliban's morality patrols. The *Mutawwa'in* detained anyone they suspected, conducted routine torture of those who did not follow the Wahhabi style of life, harassed unmarried women in public (who did not travel outdoors with a *mahram*, a male relative to whom marriage is prohibited), among other social atrocities. The state repression in Saudi Arabia, meanwhile, dispatched the Saudi left, groups such as the Arabian Peninsula People's Union and the Voice of the Vanguard.

In October 1973 the Saudi government joined with OPEC to help raise the price of oil, an event that gained the Saudi regime legitimacy among the Arab masses. But the 1973 event, again, illustrates the Janus-face of McJihad. In 1971, when the dollar was delinked from the gold standard, the Nixon administration puzzled over strategies to exert power over the global economy. One of these strategies was a rise in the oil price which would, the Nixon administration surmised, do at least two things: put an immense squeeze on the US's two main economic competitors, Western Europe and Japan, and earn profits for the Gulf states which would, in all probability, be recycled into US financial institutions because the Gulf states did not have adequate productive capacity to absorb the petro-dollars. The elimination of capital controls in the US economy by 1974 facilitated the recycling of these petro-dollars and therefore the global enhancement of the status of the dollar as the instrument of 'hard currency'.[34] The 1973 price rise was seen in the Arab world, however, as the Saudi's independence from the US, a situation not borne out by the facts. When the US State Department announced on 13 September 1980 that the US would protect Saudi Arabia against 'all internal and external attempts to destabilize it', there should have been nothing untoward about it.

McJihad, then, is along the grain of neoliberalism: weak regulation of certain sectors of the economy, coupled with a strong repressive apparatus and with cultural nationalism intended to draw upon popular legitimacy just as the regime sells its national interests to transnational corporations. During the days of Nasser or indeed the Indian Congress Party from 1947 to 1975, the cloak of nationalism (whether pan-Arabism or Indian nationalism) enabled the regime to be the legitimate leader even as the economy did not welcome the masses into a national nirvana. With the collapse of the import-substitution agenda and with the 'there is no alternative' push to globalization, the political form that emerged to maintain the quiescence of a further impoverished citizenry was to be McJihad, the Hindu Right in India, the Muslim Right in Egypt.[35]

The gambit changed in 1979 with the revolution in Iran. Now the gendarme of the US vanished, indeed it was converted into a foe of US imperialism. Given that the regime inculcated its Shi'a roots, it appealed to the generally oppressed Shi'a across the Arab lands, from Lebanon to the eastern part of Saudi Arabia. To join in the fervor of the revolution, Hizbollah ('Army of God') groups emerged across the Arab world as the party of the Shi'a to liberate Islam from its, and working-people from their, bondage. Shi'a in Lebanon, long oppressed and disenfranchised, took to Hizbollah with enthusiasm, particularly in West Beirut that was then ruined even more. The US entry into Beirut in 1982 intensified the struggle, and Beirut was trapped between two forces impatient to shoot first and talk later, one the armed imam, the other the armed marine, both equally unwilling to understand the social interests that set them on each other's throats. In Saudi Arabia, the growth of the Shi'a rebellion was not among the wretched of the earth, but among those who lived beside the oil. Although the Saudi Shi'a comprise less than a tenth of the population of the peninsula, the Shi'a congregate in the eastern side of the province, where they number as much as forty per cent. An interest in technical and secondary education led the Shi'a to good jobs with ARAMCO in the oil bureaucracy that developed from the 1940s onwards, and between thirty and forty per cent of those who worked for ARAMCO came from the Shi'a community. This economic power led the Shi'a to demand some political power, but their attempts bore little fruit (the uprising in Qatif led by Muhammad ibn Hussein al-Harraj in 1948 was crushed). Another rising in Qatif in 1970 closed off the town for a month, and another rising in 1978 led to arrests and executions. But the real explosion took place between 3 and 5 December 1979 when the Shi'a responded to Ayatollah Khomeini's victory in Iran; the Saudi repression was severe and in its aftermath was born Saudi Hizbollah, a group that was never very large but matched the Saudi police brutality for brutality.

From the dream of pan-Arabism emerged the nightmare of Iraq as the bulwark for the Saudi cause against the revolutionary zeal of Iran and of the Shi'a minority in the Arab lands. Iraq became the forward position to exert pain on Iran to show its allies in the Hizbollah movement that their politics would not go without answer. In August 1980 the Saudis and the Iraqis concluded an agreement so that the Saudis promised the Ba'ath regime 'all the financial aid required to undertake all the necessary moves to protect its national honour'. The Iran–Iraq War (1980–89) was fought by Iraq on behalf of its US, Kuwaiti and Saudi paymasters, at a great loss of life on both sides and a great gain for the Saudis and the emirs of the oil lands. When Saddam Hussein invaded Kuwait in 1990, he did so in the belief that the US would back him because Kuwait both refused to forgo Iraq's debts incurred due to the war, and because Kuwait had begun to pump oil out of the disputed Rumailla oilfields (in Jeddah, in July 1990, the UAE, Qatar, Kuwait, Iraq and Saudi Arabia agreed to reduce oil production and raise prices, but an hour after the meeting, the Kuwaitis announced that the agreement would only last for three months – an act that created a run on the Iraqi dinar). On 25 July 1990 Saddam Hussein met with US Ambassador April Glaspie. Hussein and his foreign minister Tariq Aziz pointed out the importance of raising the price of oil. Glaspie said in response, 'We have many Americans who would like the price to rise above $25 because they are from oil-producing states'.[36] This was Saddam Hussein's green light. He moved on Kuwait the day after the US approved of the sale of $695 million worth of advanced transmission devices to Iraq.

But the opportunity posed by the situation was too great. Sami Yousif calls this analysis a 'conspiracy theory', but it is borne out by the facts: that the US set up Saddam Hussein, watched him take Kuwait and then entered a war that has allowed it to maintain a position of unmatched dominance over its allies (who require US presence) and against Japan and Germany who rely on Gulf oil for their productive capacity.[37] The US presence in the Gulf, notably in Saudi Arabia, produced much unrest in the peninsula so that in 1992 over a hundred leading clerics signed a petition to the king entitled 'Memorandum of Advice' that called for a Talibanization of Saudi Arabia and a break of ties with the US, *and for the democratization of the country*. King Fahd, in December 1992, said that 'the pulpit was only made for certain limited things', and proceeded to take away the legitimacy of many of these clerics. It was this struggle that emboldened bin Laden in his crusade against the Saudi regime, from Sudan and now from Afghanistan.

And Afghanistan poses for us another site of McJihad, a place that received in large numbers the 'lost generation' of Arab men, disheartened and unemployed in their native lands, but eager for a quest for justice – so their regimes paid for this energy to be shipped off to fight the Soviets in Afghanistan instead of at home, to destabilize the tolerance of Arabia.[38] In 1964, King Zahir Shah responded to popular pressure from his subjects with a constitution and initiated a process known as 'New Democracy'. Three main forces grew after this phase: (1) the communists (who split into two factions in 1967, Khalq [the masses] and Parcham [the flag]); (2) the Islamic populists, among whom Burhanuddin Rabbani's Jamiat-i-Islami from 1973 was the main organization (whose youth leader was the engineering student, Gulbuddin Hikmatyar); (3) constitutional reformers (such as Muhammad Daoud, cousin of Zahir Shah, whose coup of July 1973 abolished the monarchy). Daoud's consequent repression against the theocratic elements pushed them into exile from where they began, along with the Pakistani Jamaat-i-Islami and the Saudi Rabitat al-Alam al-Islami, to plot against the secular regime in Afghanistan. In 1975, for instance, the theocratic elements, led by Hikmatyar in Paktia, attempted an uprising with Pakistani assistance, but the 'Panjsher Valley incident' was promptly squashed. The first split amongst the theocratic elements occurred in the aftermath of this incident. Instability in Afghanistan, an inability of the regime to undertake genuine land reform and a capitulation to corruption led to the communist coup in 1978 (the conjunctural movement was the police's move to act against a huge demonstration; the left-wing officers in the military stopped the police with a single shot and turned over the government to Noor Mohammed Taraki, a communist professor who became the President of the Revolutionary Council of Afghanistan).

The Afghan regime was a breath of fresh air in South Central Asia. It encouraged the formation of labour unions, established a minimum wage and a progressive income tax, began to lay the ground for land reforms (it abolished rural debt), and it promulgated equal rights for men and women. In late 1978, the Taraki regime announced Decree no. 7 which aimed at a transformation of the marriage institution by attacking its monetary basis and which promoted equality between men and women. Women took leadership positions in the regime and fought social conservatives and theological fascists on various issues. Anahita Ratebzad was a major Marxist leader who sat on the Revolutionary Council; other notable leaders included Sultana Umayd, Suraya, Ruhafza Kamyar, Firouza, Dilara Mark, Professor R. S. Siddiqui, Fawjiyah Shahsawari, Dr. Aziza, Shirin Afzal and Alamat Tolqun. Ratebzad wrote the famous *Kabul Times* editorial (28 May 1978) which declared that 'Privileges which women, by right, must have are equal education, job security, health services, and free time to rear a healthy generation for building the future of the country . . . Educating and enlightening women is now the subject of close government attention'. The hope of 1978 is now lost and the pessimism must not be laid at the feet of the Taliban alone, but also of those who funded and supported the Taliban-like theocratic fascists, states such as the US, Saudi Arabia and Pakistan. Infighting within the left drew the Soviet military into Afghanistan in 1979: the valiant attempt to create a democratic state failed as a result of the inability of hegemonic states to allow the nation to come into its own.

From 1979, Afghanistan became home to violence and heroin production. Money from the most unlikely sources poured into the band of mujahideen forces located in Pakistan: the US, the Saudis (notably their general intelligence service, al-Istakhbara al-'Ama), the Kuwaitis, the Iraqis, the Libyans and the Iranians paid the theocratic elements over $1 billion per year during the 1980s (much of this money passed through the Pakistani-owned bank, the BCCI). The US–Saudi dominance in funding enabled them to choose amongst the various exiled forces – they, along with the Pakistanis, chose seven parties in 1981 that leaned more towards theocratic fascism than toward secular nationalism. One of the main financiers was the Saudi businessman, Osama bin Laden. Five years later, these seven parties joined the Union of Mujahideen of Afghanistan. Its monopoly over access to the US–Saudi link emboldened it to assassinate Professor Sayd Bahauddin Majrooh in Peshawar in 1988 when he reported that 70 per cent of the Afghan refugees wanted a return to the monarchism of Zahir Shah. Further, the Interim Islamic Government of Afghanistan called a *shura* (council) in 1989; the seven parties nominated all the representatives to the body. All liberal and left wing elements came under systematic attack from the *shura* and its armed representatives. The US–Saudi axis anointed the theocratic fascists as the heirs to Afghanistan.

With over $1 billion per year, the mujahideen and its Army of Sacrifice (Lashkar-i Isar) led by Hikmatyar (who was considered the main 'factor of stability' until 1988) built up ferocious arsenals. In 1986, they received shoulder-fired Stinger missiles that they began to fire indiscriminately into civilian areas of Afghanistan. *Asia Watch*, in 1991, reported that Hikmatyar paid his commanders for each rocket fired into Kabul. Claymore mines and other US-made anti-personnel directional fragmentation mines became a staple of the countryside. Today, about 10 million mines still litter the vales of Afghanistan (placed there by the Soviets and by the US–Saudi backed mujahideen). In 1993, the US State Department noted that landmines 'may be the most toxic and widespread pollution facing mankind'. Nevertheless, the US continues to sell mines at $ 3/mine (mines cost about $ 300–$ 1000/mine to detect and dismantle). Motorola manufactures many of the plastic components inside the mines, which makes the device undetectable by metal-detectors.

The CIA learnt to extend its resources during the Southeast Asian campaigns in the 1970s by the sale of heroin from the Golden Triangle. In Afghanistan, the Inter-Service Intelligence

(ISI) [Pakistan's CIA], the Pakistani military and civilian authorities (notably Governor Fazle Huq) and the mujahideen became active cultivators, processors and sellers of heroin (a commodity which made its Southern Asian appearance in large numbers only after 1975, and whose devastation can be gleaned in Mohsin Hamid's wonderful novel, *Moth Smoke*). The opium harvest at the Pakistan–Afghan border doubled between 1982 and 1983 (575 tons), but by the end of the decade it would grow to 800 tons. On 18 June 1986, the *New York Times* reported that the mujahideen 'have been involved in narcotics activities as a matter of policy to finance their operations'. The opium warlords worked under cover of the US–Saudi–Pakistani axis that funded their arms sales and aided the conveyance of the drugs into the European and North American markets where they account for 50 per cent of heroin sales. In 1995, CIA director of the Afghan operation, Charles Cogan said candidly: 'Our main mission was to do as much damage as possible to the Soviets. We didn't really have the resources or the time to devote to an investigation of the drug trade. . . . I don't think that we need to apologize for this. Every situation has its fallout. . . . There was fallout in terms of drugs, yes. But the main objective was accomplished. The Soviets left Afghanistan.'[39]

For corporations and for corporatized states (such as the US), an unprincipled peace allows them to extract their needs without the bother of political dissent. The Taliban briefly offered the possibility of such a peace. Formed in 1994 under the tutelage of the ISI and General Naseerullah Khan (Pakistan's Interior Minister), the Taliban comprises southern Pashtun tribes who are united by a vision of a society under Wahhabism which extols a form of Islam (*Tariqa Muhammadiya*) based on its interpretation of the Quran without the benefit of the centuries of elaboration of the complexities of the Islamic tradition. In late September 1996, Radio Kabul broadcast a statement from Mullah Agha Gulabi: 'God says that those committing adultery should be stoned to death. Anybody who drinks and says that that is not against the Quran, you have to kill him and hang his body for three days until people say this is the body of the drinker who did not obey the Quran and Allah's order.' The Taliban announced that women must be veiled and that education would cease to be available for women. Najmussahar Bangash, editor of *Tole Pashtun*, pointed out shortly thereafter that there are 40,000 war widows in Kabul alone and their children will have a hard time with their subsistence. Further, she wrote, 'if girls are not allowed to study, this will affect a whole generation'. For the US–Saudi–Unocal–Pakistan axis, geo-politics and economics made the Taliban a worthy regime for Afghanistan. Drugs, weapons and social brutalities will continue, but Washington extended a warm hand towards Mullah Mohammed Omar and the Taliban. In 1930, a US State Department 'expert' on Afghanistan offered an assessment which forms the backbone of US social attitudes and state policy towards the region: 'Afghanistan is doubtless the most fanatic hostile country in the world today'. US foreign policy continues to be driven by the dual modalities of containment (of rebellion inspired by egalitarianism) and concession (of goods which will bring profit to corporate entities). Constrained by these parameters, the US government was able to state, in 1996, 'there's on the face of it nothing objectionable at this stage'. Given this, the US sees Afghanistan simply as a *tool* in foreign policy terms and as a *mine* in economic terms. In thirty years, Afghanistan has been reduced to a 'concession' in which corporations and states vie for control over commodities and markets without concern for the dignity and destiny of the people of the region. Oil, guns, landmines and heroin are the coordinates for policy-makers, not the shadowy bodies that hang from the scaffolds like paper-flags of a nation without sovereignty.

A crucial part of this puzzle is the presence of the 'Afghan Arabs', thirty-five thousand in total from forty countries, to be part of the McJihad in Afghanistan from 1982 to 1992, and over a hundred thousand influenced and trained by it.[40] In the early 1980s, Arabs eager to join one jihad or another found themselves in Afghanistan, but the numbers did not amount to much. In

1986 the CIA Director William Casey authorized the recruitment and encouragement of *mehmeen* mujahideen for the Afghan jihad against the Soviets. Bin Laden's Offices of Service (*Maktab al Khidmat*) was one of the major avenues for recruitment of these fighters, many of whom trained in ISI-run camps while some went to remote locations in Scotland to train with the SAS.[41] According to ABC journalist John Cooley, the CIA recruited members from 'New York's Arab district in Brooklyn along Atlantic Avenue' and at 'a private rifle club in an affluent community in Connecticut' (both places from where the radical Islamists continue to recruit) and they trained them at the CIA's Farm in Virginia.[42] Bin Laden was one of those who made his way to Afghanistan, used his considerable funds to build the Khost tunnel complex in 1986 (the major CIA arms storage dump and training facility) and welcomed the Arab Afghans. 'To counter these atheist Russians, the Saudis chose me as their representative in Afghanistan', bin Laden recounted. 'I settled in Pakistan in the Afghan border region. There I received volunteers who came from the Saudi Kingdom and from all over the Arab and Muslim countries. I set up my first camp where these volunteers were trained by Pakistani and American officers. The weapons were supplied by the Americans, the money by the Saudis. I discovered that it was not enough to fight in Afghanistan, but that we had to fight on all fronts, communist or Western oppression.'[43] In 1987, units of the Arab Afghans fought some engagements in northern Afghanistan, an event that so pleased William Casey that during his next visit to Pakistan he crossed the border to personally visit the Arab Afghan camps.

When the Afghan war ended in 1992, the Arab Afghans went back home to foment jihad against their own regimes, whether in Bosnia, Kosovo, Chechnya, Philippines, Algeria, India or else Saudi Arabia. Arab Afghans (Tayyeb el Afghani, Jaffar el Afghani and Sharif al Gusmi) founded the Algerian GIA (Armed Islamic Group); Abu Hamza, an Egyptian wounded in Afghanistan, runs the London-based al-Ansar group, linked to GIA. Another

Arab Afghan (Sheikh Tariq al Fadil) formed the Yemeni Jihad, while the head of the group that conducted the Luxor attacks in November 1997, Mehat Mohammed Abdel Rahman, is also an Afghan veteran. Abu Baker Jenjalani, the head of the Abu Sayyaf Group in the Philippines, cut his teeth in the ravines of Afghanistan. The Bosnian Muslim Army, the Kosovo Liberation Army, the various factions in Chechnya, are all staffed and funded by the former Arab Afghan networks. Indeed, Michel Chossodovsky shows that the involvement of Pakistan is so deep that it 'goes far beyond supplying the Chechens with weapons and expertise; the ISI and its radical Islamic proxies are actually calling the shots in the war'.[44] And, in India, many of the *mehmeen* mujahideen in Kashmir are Arab Afghans, and many Kashmiris train among them in Pakistan and in Afghanistan. In 1996, when bin Laden returned to Afghanistan he did not know the Taliban, so the Pakistanis introduced him to them and persuaded them to turn over the Khost camps to him because, Ahmed Rashid notes, 'it wanted to retain the Khost training camps for Kashmiri militants'.[45]

That the US continues to harbour such anti-people elements as the KLA and the Bosnian Muslim Army (now as freedom fighters again), and indeed since the US–ISI–Saudis continue to fund one hand of Islamism to tolerate the excesses of Arabia, shows us that the lessons of 9/11 have not been learnt. Those who died that day are indeed 'collateral damage' not just for the bombers, but also for this line of foreign policy, and much of it has to do with energy resources.

IV. THE CONTINENT OF SLEAZE

On the continent of sleaze, all buildings have revolving doors. Diplomats, gunrunners, intelligence chiefs and others sup at the state's table and then, as if by their pure merits, they join the high table with corporate chieftains, currency shifters, assorted brigands and others. On the continent of sleaze the pipelines to the Taliban pretend to be distinguished professors and royal dignitaries. Robert Oakley began his State Department career in 1957 at the United Nations, and ends it at the National Defence University and at Unocal. Prince Turki bin Faysal didn't have to use the entrance because he was always in the big house. Destined by his birth into the British-installed Ibn Saud dynasty in Arabia, Prince Turki, like Prince Sultan, drew deep into his various talents to emerge as head of intelligence for the kingdom, and, on the side, agent for various transnational enterprises, such as the Argentinian firm Bridas. Two men of esteem, in the bogs on the continent of sleaze.

Oakley's real glory begins when the Reagan administration raised him to the post of Director of the State Department Office of Combating Terrorism in September 1984. Details of Oakley's work there are not altogether clear, but cables released through the Freedom of Information Act show us that he was involved in trying to paint Libya in as bad a light as possible regardless of the evidence, and, importantly, he was a pointman in the Iran-Contra scandal. Chapter 18 in Volume 1 of the Lawrence Walsh-authored *Report of the Independent Counsel for Iran Contra Matters* (released on 4 August 1993) notes one incident of Oakley's involvement: in November 1985, Oliver North had a hard time with clearances for the Israeli effort to ship US-made HAWK missiles to Iran. Retired Air Force Major General Richard Secord was unable to get North the clearances to act, so North went to Oakley, then director of counter-terrorism. North said that he was 'completely up front' with Oakley that the cargo for the plane was weapons and the transit was according to the October 1984 Boland Amendment passed by Congress (to cut off aid to the Contras of Nicaragua). According to Oakley's testimony to the FBI (302, 11/14/91) 'North said he needed to get a plane into the first European country in order to ship arms to Iran'. Oakley agreed with North and contacted CIA European chief Duane 'Dewey' Clarridge. Clarridge was informed that the State Department was 'aware of the operation and that Clarridge should contact the foreign minister of the first European country for assistance'.

In 1987 Clarridge was formally reprimanded for his role in

the Iran-Contra affair, and he was forced out of the CIA. North who was convicted in 1989, but then pardoned due to his immunity at the hearings, went on for a quixotic run to become the Senator from Virginia in 1994. He is now another right-wing talk show host.

Robert Oakley, currently Distinguished Fellow at the Institute for National Strategic Studies, National Defence University, went from strength to strength. He was named as Ambassador to Pakistan in August 1988 and served as a pointman in the mujahideen jihad against the People's Democratic Republic of Afghanistan and the Soviet army therein. In fact in the lead-up to a brutal two month-long battle in November 1988 (in which five thousand died), Oakley sat with senior Pakistani military officials to plan the battle).[46] This was an education in the front-lines: from illegal gun running to Iran, he moved to the promotion of jihad in Pakistan, where Oakley aided the hard line Hikmatyar and, in addition, cultivated links with those who would become the Taliban.[47]

Perhaps most crucially, the Pakistani post allowed Oakley to work with Prince Turki bin Faysal, head of the Saudi Arabian intelligence from 1977 to 1 September 2001 and pointman for his government in the mujahideen jihad (indeed he knew Osama bin Laden then, since both these men of the Saudi elite had come to Afghanistan). Prince Turki Faysal is a very influential player in the Saudi ruling elite and a major shaper of policy. Like Oakley, Turki Faysal's major links appeared to have been with the more hardcore jihadis, people such as the Taliban and the Hikmaytar crew. But, after the war, in their new line of work, Oakley and Turki Faysal sit on different sides of the corporate table.

With the collapse of the Soviet Union, the vast oil and natural gas treasures of Central Asia came back into the focus of the vast transnational energy monopolies. The Gulf War of 1991 was about the problem of oil consumption by the US population (Energy Secretary James Watkins' February 1991 letter made this plain: 'as events in the Persian Gulf have demonstrated so aptly, we must reduce our dependence on imported oil from unstable regions. This will require both reducing our overall dependence on oil, particularly in the transportation sector, and increasing domestic production in an environmentally sound manner'. The game for the 1.5 million acres of the Arctic National Wildlife Refuge was already on by then). But the Fifth Afghan War is about something else; indeed it is not about US domestic consumption. It appears that the Afghan War is about the ability of US-based transnational corporate power, about its ability to leverage access to deals (here with the Afghans) to penetrate markets (the natural gas and oil crisis of South Asia). The Central Asian oil and natural gas fields are vast (with Kazakhstan now being the fifth largest oil reserve in the world).

Two weeks after 9/11, Chevron's subsidiary Tengizchevroil finished an oil pipeline from Tengiz oil field in western Kazakhstan to the Russian port of Novorossiysk on the Black Sea. This pipeline will feed Western Europe with oil from what might end up as the fifth largest oil state in the world (and, crucially, outside OPEC's ambit). The Tengiz pipeline is only one of many that sully the geopolitics of the region. Another one, pressing for the Afghan problem, is the 890-mile pipeline from Dauletabad gas fields in eastern Turkmenistan through Afghanistan into Pakistan. This multi-billion dollar project has two multinationals on the warpath, Unocal from the US, and Bridas from Argentina. Both hired Saudis and Americans to negotiate with the Taliban, who continuously played one off against the other to increase their own percentage of the margins. Unocal, recently denied Myanmar's oil market, is eager for the project and a US-friendly regime in Afghanistan may help it clinch the deal. Zahir Shah, former King of Afghanistan, has lived in Rome since 1973 as a pensioner of a gulf state whose name he will not reveal; perhaps the investment made in him by the unnamed state will eventually come to fruition if he comes to power alongside the notorious Northern Alliance (whose terror in Kabul in the mid-1990s offers a harbinger of what is to come).

Just as no one is interested in the Uzbek army regulars who

trained in the mid-west, no-one seems to care about Unocal's project to train Afghan workers and teachers at the University of Nebraska (in November 1997, Unocal paid close to a million dollars for the Afghan Studies Center at the University to train over four hundred Afghans in various pipeline construction skills). Or, finally, no one seems interested in the US tours organized by Unocal for the Taliban (and facilitated by Pakistan's ISI who held up the visas of the Taliban tour which was to have gone, courtesy of Bridas, to Argentina).

And few of us care that distinguished professors like Oakley joined with the notorious Henry Kissinger, and the Saudi Delta Oil Company (whose boss, Badr al Aiban, has the ear of King Faud) to lobby the Taliban on behalf of Unocal, just as Prince Turki Faysal was Bridas' pointman with the Taliban. When the Taliban took power in 1996, the head of Unocal was overjoyed, and he speculated that a stable central government may reduce the cost of the pipeline by half; indeed, Marty Miller of Unocal tried to convince the factions that the pipeline was a conflict resolution process. When this did not work, some speculated that Unocal gave covert support to the Taliban to push what is today the Northern Alliance away from the area where the pipeline is projected to run.[48]

When Clinton bombed Afghanistan on 20 August 1998, the Unocal deal ended. But hope emerged on 29 April 1999 when the energy ministers from Afghanistan, Pakistan and Turkmenistan met to pledge their commitment to the tripartite gas pipeline project. It is around this time that King Zahir Shah comes under pressure to meet with the Northern Alliance and start talking about a Loya Jigra, an elder's council. The unnamed Gulf state that pensioned the poor old man for these three decades perhaps called in its debt. He was put on a fuel's errand. That Hamid Karzai is loyal to the ex-King and that he is close to the US establishment bespeaks the trend toward a capitulation to the oil barons.

Hastily, after 9/11, Unocal put the following note on their website: 'Unocal has received inquires about a previously proposed pipeline that, if built, would have crossed a part of Afghanistan. We withdrew from that project in 1998, and do not have, nor plan to have, any projects in that country. We do not support the Taliban in any way whatsoever.'

Under pressure from 9/11, this has to be the official position. But we should not forget the testimony of John Maresca, International head of Unocal, on 12 February 1998. Certainly this is before the US bombed Afghanistan in August, but it allows us access to the way Unocal has framed the importance of Afghanistan. Here is Maresca:

'The Caspian region contains tremendous untapped hydrocarbon reserves, much of them located in the Caspian Sea basin itself. Proven natural gas reserves within Azerbaijan, Uzbekistan, Turkmenistan and Kazakhstan equal more than 236 trillion cubic feet. The region's total oil reserves may reach more than 60 billion barrels of oil – enough to service Europe's oil needs for 11 years. Some estimates are as high as 200 billion barrels. In 1995, the region was producing only 870,000 barrels per day (44 million tons per year [Mt/y]). By 2010, Western companies could increase production to about 4.5 million barrels a day (Mb/d) – an increase of more than 500 per cent in only 15 years. If this occurs, the region would represent about five per cent of the world's total oil production, and almost 20 per cent of oil produced among non-OPEC countries. One major problem has yet to be resolved: how to get the region's vast energy resources to the markets where they are needed. There are few, if any, other areas of the world where there can be such a dramatic increase in the supply of oil and gas to the world market. The solution seems simple: build a "new" Silk Road. Implementing this solution, however, is far from simple. The risks are high, but so are the rewards.'

The most logical path for the pipeline would be due south through Iran, but Maresca rejects this and settles on Afghanistan:

'The only other possible route option is across Afghanistan, which has its own unique challenges. The country has been involved in bitter warfare for almost two decades. The territory across which the pipeline would extend is controlled by the Taliban, an Islamic movement that is not recognized as a government by most other nations. From the outset, we have made it clear that construction of our proposed pipeline cannot begin until a recognized government is in place that has the confidence of governments, lenders and our company. In spite of this, a route through Afghanistan appears to be the best option with the fewest technical obstacles. It is the shortest route to the sea and has relatively favourable terrain for a pipeline. The route through Afghanistan is the one that would bring Central Asian oil closest to Asian markets and thus would be the cheapest in terms of transporting the oil.'

Iran is not off the table as yet, because in early December 2001, after a meeting with US Secretary of State Colin Powell, Kazakh President Nursultan Nazarbayev said that Iran is the logical route for the pipeline and that the US 'bypassed the issue on purpose' not for economic reasons but because of their antipathy to Iran. Powell was diplomatic when he said that 'nothing in the post-September 11 [climate] suggests that we rethink [the pipeline projects that skirt Iran because they] seem to me to indicate that there will be stability with respect to the supply of fuel.' In other words, Afghanistan is the only route that the US will sanctify.

In December 2000 the US Government Energy Information Factsheet on Afghanistan reported: 'Afghanistan's significance from an energy standpoint stems from its geographical position as a potential transit route for oil and natural gas exports from Central Asia to the Arabia Sea. This potential includes proposed multi-billion dollar oil and gas export pipelines through Afghanistan.'[49] The region in question, we are told, bears oil and natural gas resources worth $4 billion, a vast ransom. In 1998, Richard Cheney (then head of Halliburton, a major oil player, and now Vice President of the US) said, 'I cannot think of a time when we have had a region emerge as suddenly to become as strategically significant as the Caspian.' Since the US imports just over half its crude oil and since this figure seems unlikely to decrease, and that the Saudi fields may not run forever, the possibility of more oil and natural gas is an immense incentive for a war against the planet.

On the continent of sleaze, the military men and the corporate men spill blood to put a 'recognized government in place that has the confidence of governments, lenders and our company'. Democracy is irrelevant. Distinguished professors and intelligence heads gather to help feed our addiction to oil. As the bombs fall in passive voice, the active voices of corporate greed and military macho have begun to ring. The bombs are not retaliation for 9/11; they are a 911 for the continuation of capitalist imperialism against the active will of most of us on the planet.

5

Afterword

Afterwards, we'll hear the details of this war shrouded by the US–UK military's close scrutiny of the news. We heard that the military did its best to protect civilian lives, but already (on 10 December 2001) Professor Marc Herold of the University of New Hampshire calculated that the minimum number of civilians killed by the US bombs couldn't be less than 3500. We heard that the Northern Alliance backed by the US aircrafts and Special Forces routed the Taliban, but we may soon hear that the Taliban lost steam when most of their commanders switched sides as opportunistically as they had joined them in the mid-1990s. We may someday hear that the cluster bombs devastated the fields and irrigation channels of the Afghan peasantry, many of whom will probably sow that easy to grow weed, opium, to make ends meet and thereby fuel a harvest of grief for working-class people in Europe, the US, and in South Asia (increasingly a major market for heroin). Afterwards, we may hear about all this, and only from dissident journalists muzzled during the conflict, from the memoirs of CIA officials who are eager to write themselves into history books, or else from the words of the Afghan people told to those of their fellows angry for the devastation wrought on their land.

Already the question of when to declare a victory has befuddled the US administration. Secretary of State Colin Powell, hesitant to enter the conflict in the first place, declared by the end of the second week of December that the al-Qa'ida had been 'destroyed' and removed from Afghanistan. 'This is the last day of the al-Qa'ida in Afghanistan', noted the warlord Hazrat Ali as a broken detachment of al-Qa'ida fighters surrendered in the White Mountains near Tora Bora. But, on his return flight from Afghanistan where he consulted with Hamid Karzai, Defence Secretary Rumsfeld said, 'The fact of the matter is, as Secretary Powell knows well, there are still any number of al-Qa'ida loose in that country. That is why we are there, that is why we are chasing them, that is why we are bombing.' As 2001 winded down, the US bombers based in northern Afghanistan and Uzbekistan continued to pummel the Afghan countryside.

The disagreement offers us insight into the political campaign waged by the Rumsfeld wing of US imperialism: to find any reason to continue a US presence in the region, to cement the US bases set up in northern Afghanistan. The United States went to war in Afghanistan to gain a beachhead in Central Asia, a frontier post from where it will be able to threaten all of Asia with its immense military might. A bomber would take several hours to scramble from Diego Garcia to reach the heart of India, or Central Asia, but from Afghanistan the flight time is now much reduced. Interactions with the US of all kinds will now be conducted in the shadow of this military fact in much the same way as the US presence in East Asia constrains the political activities of that region. If the war is over, as Powell put it, then the US should leave. If the war continues for a few more weeks, even months, it will help the US justify its presence alongside the international force that may enter Afghanistan under the UN flag.

All eyes are on bin Laden, and so there is silence on the US activities in the north of the country and in neighbouring Uzbekistan. Of bin Laden, Rear Admiral John Stufflebeam noted that 'It's very difficult to see where he's at and certainly impossible to predict where he'll be'. It seems clear that he is not in Afghanistan and he may certainly have gone anywhere via Pakistan. Gul Agha Sherzai of the government of Kandahar told the press that Pakistani smugglers charged fugitive al-Qa'ida fighters $5,000 per head for safe passage into Pakistan – bin Laden may have gone that route or else left Afghanistan before the war began. This we will only learn afterwards. As Stufflebeam noted, 'we're pretty good at being able to describe where he's been', but unable to find out where he has gone.

The contradictions of imperialist globalization will continue to turn people into the willing agents of bin Laden-style reaction if there is no rebirth of the left in the zones where bin Ladenism attracts its adherents. If the left does not garner the chaff of globalization into a mighty force, then terrorism will continue and give the right more reasons to hamper the creativity of human beings. Che Guevara, the Argentinian doctor who was a main force in the Cuban revolution, wrote, 'Terrorism is a measure that is generally ineffective and indiscriminate in its effect, since it often makes victims of innocent people and destroys a large number of lives that would be valuable to the revolution. Besides it hinders all the more or less legal or semi-clandestine contact with the masses and makes impossible unification for actions that will be necessary at a critical moment.' Guevara repeated, independently, the words of our own revolutionary martyr, Bhagat Singh, words written three decades before Che. Bhagat Singh, in jail, wrote that non-violent political organization is 'indispensable for mass movements', and he reserved the right to defend violent acts against imperialist institutions 'only in times of terrible necessity'. Acts of terror against the people, then, are not only morally indefensible, but they are also politically juvenile. Powerlessness, too, grows out of the barrel of a gun.

Notes

1. INTRODUCTION

[1] Of course the 1839 war was not the first to wrack the Afghan region, but it was the first significant invasion since the formation of the kingdom by Ahmad Shah Durrani, in the aftermath of the assassination of the maverick Nadir Shah in 1747 (Durrani, from the title given to Ahmed Shah by his fellow chiefs of Kandahar – *Dur-i-Duran*, 'Pearl of the Age'). This is the same Ahmed Shah who vanquished a well-tested Maratha force on the plains of Panipat on 6 January 1761. The kingdom of the Durranis fought many wars on its frontier with the Persians over the demarcation of a boundary, but these battles do not qualify as invasions.

[2] Zahir Shah himself was not averse to an alliance with fascism, as reported by Tariq Ali. Here is a document from the German Foreign Office (3 October 1940), from State Secretary Weizsacker to the German Legation in Kabul: 'The Afghan Minister called on me on September 30 and conveyed greetings from his Minister President and the War Minister, as well as their good wishes for a favourable outcome of the war. He inquired whether German aims in Asia coincided with Afghan hopes; he alluded to the oppression of Arab countries and referred to the 15 million Afghans [Pashtuns] who were forced to suffer on Indian territory. My statement that Germany's goal was the liberation of the peoples of the region referred to, who were under the British yoke, as well as the restoration of their rights, was received with satisfaction by the Afghan Minister. He stated that justice for Afghanistan would be created only when the country's frontier had been extended to the Indus; this would also apply if India should secede from Britain. . . . The Afghan remarked that Afghanistan had given proof of her loyal attitude by vigorously resisting English pressure to break off relations with Germany. Today

he wanted to present Afghanistan's wishes as a matter of precaution, but he requested strict secrecy; he called a fulfillment of these wishes a matter for the future.' Tariq Ali, 'The Afghan King and the Nazis', *Counterpunch*, 30 November 2001.

3 *Washington Post*, 20 June 1986.

4 This list is carefully drawn-up, based on a close analysis of US military documents and State Department papers. For Kosovo, see Noam Chomsky, *The New Military Humanism: Lessons from Kosovo* (Monroe: Common Courage, 1999); for the 'War on Drugs', see Richard Friman, *NarcoDiplomacy: Exporting the US War on Drugs* (Ithaca: Cornell University Press, 1996); for the encirclement of China, see Vijay Prashad, 'On the Periphery of Asia: Thoughts on US Imperialism', *The Marxist*, XV: 2–3 (April–September 1999); for weapons in space, see Karl Grossman, *Weapons in Space* (New York: Seven Stories Press, 2000).

CHAPTER 2. 9/11

1 Boris Kagarlitsky, 'Bin Laden? Better Be Right', *Moscow Times*, 18 September 2001.

2 Youssef Bodansky, *Bin Laden. The Man Who Declared War on America* (New York: Forum, 2001), p. 14.

3 Robert Fisk, 'This Loose Conjecture is Unlikely to Cut Much Ice with the Arab Nations', *The Independent*, 5 October 2001.

4 Government of the United Kingdom, *Responsibility for the terrorist atrocities in the United States, 11 September 2001* (4 October 2001).

5 All this is solipsistic, because we know that the US engagement in Afghanistan will not alter international norms, since these laws are designed for the world to follow and for the US to break. While the US denounces the use of military tribunals for the trial of its citizens in foreign lands, President Bush authorized the use of these military courts to try suspected terrorists who are in the US on legal visas – another act of hypocrisy that calls into doubt the US state's commitment to international legality.

6 Seymour M. Hersh, 'King's Ransom: How Vulnerable are the Saudi Royals?' *The New Yorker*, 22 October 2001.

7 Anthony H. Cordesman, *Saudi Arabia Enters the 21st Century: Politics and Internal Stability* (Washington, DC: Center for International and Strategic Studies) 1 August 2001.

8 *Wall Street Journal*, 26 December 1995, p. A-7.

9 The ground for much of this is laid out in *Jane's Intelligence Review*, June 2001, pp. 34–35.

10 Ahmed Rashid, *Taliban* (New Haven: Yale University Press, 2000), p. 34.

11 Ibid., pp. 165–66.

12 Ibid., p. 178.

13 In 1995, when the Hikmatyar government fell in Kabul, the Taliban 'handed control of training camps in Afghanistan over to JUI [Jama'at-i-Ulema-i-Islam] factions'. *International Press Services*, 22 August 1995.

14 For example, 'Making a Symbol of Terror', *Newsweek*, 1 March 1999.

15 Alexandra Richard, 'La CIA Aurait Rencontré Ben Laden en Juillet', *Le Figaro*, 31 October 2001, p. 2.

[16] Jonathan Steele, et al., 'Threat of US Strikes Passed to Taliban Weeks Before NY Attacks', *The Guardian*, 21 September 2001.

[17] In the context of the war, Huntington's 1993 article for *Foreign Affairs* was well critiqued by Edward W. Said, 'The Clash of Ignorance', *The Nation*, 22 October 2001.

CHAPTER 3. WAR IN PASSIVE VOICE

[1] Nikki R. Keddie, *Religion and Politics in Iran: Shi'ism from Quietism to Revolution* (New Haven: Yale University Press, 1983); Val Moghadam, 'Socialism or Anti-Imperialism? The Left and Revolution in Iran', *New Left Review*, 161 (November/December 1987) as well as 'The Revolution and the Regime: Populism, Islam and the State in Iran', *Social Compass*, 36: 4 (1989).

[2] Pirouz Mojtahed-Zadeh, 'Geopolitics and Reform Under Khatami', *Global Dialogue*, 3: 2–3 (Spring/Summer 2001), p. 60.

[3] Jeromin Zettelmeyer, 'The Uzbek Growth Puzzle', *IMF Staff Papers*, 46: 3 (September/December 1999).

[4] Ahmed Rashid, 'The Taliban: Exporting Extremism', *Foreign Affairs* (November/December 1999).

[5] C.J. Chivers, 'In Home Called Base of Jihad Teacher, the Lessons of Terror', *The New York Times*, 1 December 2001, p. B1.

[6] Aijaz Ahmad, *Lineages of the Present* (London: Verso, 2000), p. 308.

[7] Pakistan has had a strained relationship with Afghanistan since the creation of the former state. Between 29 March and 1 April 1955, the states withdrew diplomatic contact as anti-Pakistani demonstrations closed down Kabul. Again on 26 April 1961, over the boundary, relations collapsed between the states, only to be re-established on 29 May 1963 after a communiqué by both powers created what we would now call confidence building measures, but did not come up with any solution to various disputes.

[8] Maharaj Kaul, 'Afghanistan', FOIL listserver (16 November 2001).

[9] Rashid, *Taliban*, pp. 27–29.

[10] *Wall Street Journal* (Asian Edition), 23 October 2000.

[11] Farhan Bokhari, 'The IMF in Pakistan', *Financial Times*, 2 September 1999.

[12] Rashid, *Taliban*, p. 89.

[13] Arif Jamal, 'Almi Tanzeem Almi Sunnat', *The News* [Pakistan], 10 June 2001.

[14] Praveen Swami and Anupama Katakam, 'The Tale Documents Tell', *Frontline*, 18: 15 (21 July–3 August 2001); 'The Shiv Sena's Games', *Frontline*, 18: 16, (4–17 August 2001); 'A Hysterical Campaign', *Frontline*, 18: 17 (18–31 August 2001).

[15] *Damning Verdict. Report of the Justice Srikrisha Commission* (Mumbai: Sabrang, n. d.), p. 1.

[16] On which, and so much more, see Praveen Swami, *The Kargil War. Chronicle of a War Foretold* (New Delhi: LeftWord, 1999).

[17] Manoj Joshi, *The Lost Rebellion. Kashmir in the Nineties* (New Delhi: Penguin, 1998), p. 17.

[18] Zafaryab Ahmed, 'Maudoodi's Islamic State', *Islam, Politics and the State: The Pakistan Experience*, edited by Asghar Khan (London: Zed, 1985).

[19] John F. Burns, 'Errant Cluster Bomb Leaves Danger Behind, UN Says', *New York Times*, 25 October 2001.

[20] Tim Weiner, 'US Bombs Hit 3 Towns, Afghans Say; Pentagon Denies It', *New York Times*, 2 December 2001, p. B2.

[21] Two pieces by Richard Lloyd Parry: 'US Bombs Hit Wrong Target for Second Time in Two Days' and 'US Afghan Allies Were Bombed as they Slept', both in the *Independent*, 3 December 2001.

[22] Most of my details are from Sven Lindquist's wonderful *The History of Bombing* (New York: The New Press, 2001).

[23] Ibid., p. 48.

[24] Ibid., p. 74.

[25] Ibid., p. 96.

[26] Ibid., p. 109.

[27] Bruce Cumings, *Korea's Place in the Sun. A Modern History* (New York: Norton, 1997), p. 296.

[28] Lindquist, *The History of Bombing*, p. 31.

[29] Aziz Haniffa, 'US turned Afghanistan into a minefield: Human Rights Watch', *India Abroad*, 30 November 2001, p. 6.

[30] 'I think as we sort through the evidence, in my judgment', said Larry Johnson, a regular counter terrorism expert at the US State Department, 'this has the hallmarks of Islamic ties' (CNN, 20 April 1995). He was soon to be belied by the evidence.

[31] On 8 December, in an address in Farsi, Hamid Karzai said, 'We pay tribute to the role of Iran in Afghanistan and hope for the continuity of amicable and brotherly relations between Kabul and Tehran'. Karzai, in this manner, hoped to circumvent any Rabbani–Iran move on the cabinet.

[32] As reported by Ahmed Rashid, 'Hamid Karzai Moves from Lightweight to Heavyweight in Afghan Politics', 10 December 2001.

[33] Alfonso Rojo, 'Los taliban persiguen al nuevo hombre de la CIA', *El Mundo*, 3 November 2001 and Doug Ireland, 'History Lessons. What Bush Should Have Learnt From the Cold War', *In These Times*, 7 December 2001.

[34] The interested reader may study Amnesty International's reports published in 1995 on major abuses by Rabbani's Jamait-i-Islami, Hikmatyar's Hezb-i-Islami, Dostam's Junbest-i-Melli Islami and Hezb-i-Wahdat: (1) *Afghanistan: International Responsibility for Human Rights Disaster* (AI Index ASA 11/09/95) and (2) *Women in Afghanistan: A Human Rights Catastrophe* (AI Index ASA 11/03/95).

[35] Robert Fitch, *The Assassination of New York* (New York: Verso, 1993), p. 100.

[36] Robert Reich, 'How Did Spending Become Our Patriotic Duty?' *Washington Post*, 23 September 2001.

[37] Robert B. Zoellick, 'Countering Terror with Trade', *Washington Post*, 20 September 2001.

CHAPTER 4. THE TOLERANCE OF ARABIA

[1] Quoted in Fouad Ajami, *The Dream Palace of the Arabs* (New York: Vintage, 1998), p. 126.

[2] There was a constant refrain in the media that the US troops (and particularly air

force pilots bemoaned the lack of 'targets' given their immense military superiority. For example, James Dao, 'The New Air War: Fewer Pilots, More Hits and Scarcer Targets', *The New York Times*, 29 November 2001, p. B1.

3 We need to take into consideration the prevalent mythology that comes to us at the origins of the European colonization of the Americas – the myth of innocence. The persecuted Europeans flee the guiles of Old Europe to make a place that does not replicate its complexity, deviousness and intrigue. They arrive in the Americas, wide-eyed and curious, desperate for a new life. These settlers do not care for the artificiality of feudal manners so they inaugurate a world of forthrightness, frankness and independence. Hardy, courageous, tough – this is the self-image of the colonial settlers. The genocide of the Amerindians, the slavery of peoples from Africa, the widespread disruption of anti-colonialism in the name of anti-communism – this is the legacy that is lost by America's innocent amnesia. In March 1968, the National Advisory Commission on Civil Disorders tendered its report on the uprisings of the decade, and it offered an indictment that covers this general sense of amnesia: 'What white Americans have never fully understood – but what the Negro can never forget – is that white society is deeply implicated in the ghetto. White institutions created it, white institutions maintain it, and white society condones it'. The US state's inability to deal with racism is certainly a consequence of the innocent amnesia of whiteness, the grave desire to represent racism as the touchiness of the oppressed or as the province of an isolated group of Aryanists. The history of white privilege is actively forgotten, that history of white suburbanization through federal assistance, of the creation of white equity, and of the immense amount of values appropriated without wages from a determinate set of peoples whose descendents for the most part are capital poor.

4 It is important to note that the interests of the USSR and the national communist parties did not always fall into line. Two examples of that in the Arab world include the USSR's friendship with Saddam Hussein as he went after the Iraqi Communist movement between 1969 and 1972, and the USSR's support of Colonel Ja'far al-Numayri just as he jailed Sudanese Communist Party chair 'Abd al-Khaliq Mahjub in 1971. On Iraq, see Hanna Batatu, *The Old Social Classes and the Revolutionary Movement in Iraq* (Princeton: Princeton University Press, 1978), and on Sudan, see El Mahdawi, 'Dark Days in The Sudan', *African Communist*, 47 (1971).

5 Reuven Paz, 'The Saudi Fatwa Against Suicide Terrorism', *Peacewatch*, 323 (2 May 2001).

6 Kwame Nkrumah, *Neocolonialism. The Last Stage of Imperialism* (New York: International Publishers, 1965), p. xi.

7 The most informative study on the Saudi dynasty is by Saïd K. Aburish, *The Rise, Corruption and Coming Fall of the House of Saud* (New York: St. Martin's, 1994). The quote from Glubb Pasha is on p. 24.

8 The story is well told in the classic work of Arabism, George Antonius, *The Arab Awakening* (New York: Capricorn Books, 1965).

9 Musa Budeiri, *The Palestine Communist Party, 1919–1948. Arab and Jew in the Struggle for Internationalism* (London: Ithaca Press, 1979) and Selma Botman, *The Rise of Egyptian Communism, 1939–1970* (Syracuse: Syracuse University Press,

1988).

10 Batutu, *The Old Social Classes*, p. 569.

11 Ibid., p. 465.

12 James Risen, 'Secrets of History. The CIA in Iran – A Special Report', *New York Times*, 16 April 2000, p. 1.

13 William Cleveland, *The Making of an Arab Nationalist: Ottomanism and Arabism in the Life and Thought of Sati al-Husri* (Princeton: Princeton University Press, 1971).

14 Marie-Christine Aulas, 'State and Ideology in Republican Egypt, 1952–1982', *State and Ideology in the Middle East and Pakistan*, edited by Fred Halliday and Hamza Alavi (New York: Monthly Review Press, 1988), p. 134.

15 Quoted in Samir al-Khalil, *Republic of Fear. The Politics of Modern Iraq* (Berkeley: University of California Press, 1989), p. 191 and p. 226.

16 Roy Mottahedeh, *The Mantle of the Prophet. Religion and Politics in Iran* (New York: Pantheon, 1985), p. 130.

17 Aburish, *Rise, Corruption and Coming Fall*, p. 161.

18 'Islam, Democracy, the State and the West', *Middle East Policy*, 1: 3 (1992), p. 52.

19 Aburish, *Rise, Corruption and Coming Fall*, p. 49.

20 Quoted in Mai Yamani, *Changed Identities. The Challenge of the New Generation in Saudi Arabia* (London: Royal Institute for International Affairs, 2000), p. 39.

21 I tracked the Turkish state's violence against the left Kurds in 'Hot Turkey: The US Authorized Kurdish Massacre', *Economic and Political Weekly*, 12–19 October 1996.

22 For more on these maladies, see Ahmad El Khory, 'Nationalism and Class Struggle in the Arab World', *Monthly Review*, 22: 3 (July–August 1970).

23 Aulas, 'State and Ideology', pp. 141–43.

24 M. Abdel-Fadil, *Development, Income Distribution and Social Change in Rural Egypt, 1952–1970* (Cambridge: Cambridge University Press, 1975), p. 49; R. Mabro and S. Radwan, *The Industrialization of Egypt, 1939–1973* (Oxford: Clarendon Press, 1976), p. 239.

25 Benjamin Barber, *Jihad Versus McWorld* (New York: Ballatine, 1996). My thoughts on this problem in relation to West Asia benefited from Joel Beinin, 'Late Capitalist Crisis, Middle East Oil and Political Islam', *Between the Lines*, 1: 6 (April 2001).

26 Richard P. Mitchell, *The Society of the Muslim Brothers* (New York: Oxford University Press, 1993).

27 Mahmud A. Faksh, *The Future of Islam in the Middle East* (Westport: Praeger, 1997), p. 45.

28 'To organize a communist group', said the former communist leader Ibrahim Nugud, 'we had to find safe houses. To organize an Islamic political group, you can meet openly five times a day [at prayer time], in the mosque'. Quoted in Peter Ford, 'Challenging Regimes, Koran in Hand', *Christian Science Monitor*, 21 April 1993, p. 11.

29 Hasan Hanafi, 'The Relevance of the Islamic Alternative in Egypt', *Arab Studies Quarterly*, 4 (Spring 1982), p. 63.

30 Fouad Ajami, 'Retreat from Economic Nationalism: The Political Economy of

Sadat's Egypt', *Journal of Arab Affairs*, 1 (October 1981), pp. 27–52.

[31] Caryle Murphy, 'Poverty Breeds Despair in Egypt', *Washington Post*, 15 July 1994, p. A14.

[32] 'Now all of Venezuela is oil', wrote the author Arturo Uslar Pietri. 'Not oil sown and transformed into harvests and factories, as it could and should have been; but oil flooding over and carrying away houses, plants and cattle in its path'. Guillermo Morón, *A History of Venezuela* (New York: Roy, 1963), p.199.

[33] John Rossant, 'Are the Sands about to Shift under Saudi Arabia?' *Business Week*, 15 February 1993, and Nora Boustany, 'At Saudis' Rich Table, the Alien Taste of Austerity', *Washington Post*, 13 August 1994, p. A1.

[34] Peter Gowan, *The Global Gamble. Washington's Faustian Bid for World Dominance* (London: Verso, 1999), pp. 21–22 and A.A. Kuburi and S. Mansur, 'The Political Economy of Middle Eastern Oil', *Political Economy and the Changing Global Order*, edited by G.R.D. Underhill and R. Stubbs (London: Macmillan, 1994).

[35] Prakash Karat, 'Liberalization and Hindutva: New Threats to National Unity', *Social Scientist*, 27: 9–10 (September–October 1999).

[36] *New York Times*, 23 September 1991.

[37] Sami Yousif, 'The Iraqi–US War: A Conspiracy Theory', *The Gulf War and the New World Order*, edited by Haim Bresheeth and Nira Yuval-Davis (London: Zed, 1991).

[38] The phrase 'lost generation' is from Rachid al-Ghannouchi, leader of the Islamic Tendency Movement in Tunisia, as quoted in Linda Jones, 'Portrait of Rashid al-Ghannouchi', *Middle East Report*, July–August 1988, p. 20.

[39] Quoted in Alfred McCoy, 'Drug Fallout: The CIA's Forty Year Complicity in the Narcotics Trade', *The Progressive*, 1 August 1997.

[40] *Washington Post*, 19 July 1992.

[41] Ken Connor, *Ghost Force. The Secret History of the SAS* (London: Orion). Keenie-Meenie Services, a part of the British security firm Control Risks, and staffed by ex-SAS members from Rhodesia and South Africa worked among the jihadis in Afghanistan.

[42] John Cooley, *Unholy Wars. Afghanistan, America and International Terrorism* (London: Pluto).

[43] Quoted in Rashid, *Taliban*, p. 132.

[44] Michel Chossodovsky, 'Who is Osama bin Laden?', www.globalresearch.ca, 13 September 2001.

[45] Rashid, *Taliban*, p. 139.

[46] 'Pakistanis Report Ordering Attacks by Afghan Rebels', *New York Times*, 23 April 1989.

[47] Kurt Kohbeck, *Holy War, Unholy Victory: Eyewitness to the CIA's Secret War in Afghanistan*, 1993.

[48] Ahmed Rashid, 'Pipe Dreams', *The Herald* (Pakistan), October 1997, p. 50.

[49] These details are in Sitaram Yechury, 'America, Oil and Afghanistan', *The Hindu*, 13 October 2001.